THE CIRCLE OF LIFE

*The Process of Sexual Recovery
Workbook*

THE CIRCLE OF LIFE

The Process of Sexual Recovery Workbook

*Guide Thru the
12 Steps for Sex Addicts*

By

KJ NIVIN
*Anonymous Recovering
Sex Addict*

Published by
KJ Nivin
kjnivin@yahoo.com
Virginia Beach, VA 23451
The Circle Of Life

The Process of Sexual Recovery

Workbook

ISBN: 1449931014
EAN-13: 9781449931018

Updated July 2011

Table of Contents

Disclaimer

The Circle of Life is written *"by* sex addicts *for* sex addicts" and is not intended to replace professional counseling or professional medical help. This is written from a sponsor's viewpoint. The intention of this book is to *aid* anyone seeking help for recovery from sexual addiction and compulsive sexual behavior. The sole purpose of *The Circle of Life* is to bring awareness to and assist in recovery from sexual addiction through the introduction of sponsorship and by encouraging those affected to work the 12 Steps. There are no guarantees implied or otherwise stated herein. Sexual Addiction is a disease with no known cure but this compulsive addiction may be arrested and managed.

The Circle of Life has no affiliation with any 12 Step organizations. These organizations are autonomous and are not affiliated with any outside entities. The people who developed this workbook are not professional counselors or doctors. We are recovering sex addicts who have found, by working the 12 Steps for sexual addiction with a sponsor, and by attending sexual recovery meetings, that we have been able to live a more normal life when it comes to sex. We are sharing our experience, strength and hope so that others may benefit.

It may be necessary to seek professional help as well.

––––––––––––––––––––––––––––

Note: Alcoholics Anonymous, nor is any other 12 Step programs of recovery (to include DA, NA, GA, SLAA, SAA, SA, RCA etc), affiliated with this publication, or that it has read and/or endorses the contents thereof. A.A. is a program of recovery from alcoholism only-inclusion of the Steps in this publication, or use in any other non-A.A. context, does not imply otherwise. Additionally, while A.A. is a spiritual program, A.A. is not a religious program. Thus, A.A. is not affiliated or allied with any sect, denomination, or specific religious belief.

––––––––––––––––––––––––––––

ACKNOWLEDGEMENTS

To my family April, Kurt and Ben for their patience and support; To My Big Sis Shirley

To my mother Lue who inspired me to start my recovery by her example of joining Al-Anon to overcome the affects of addiction in her life;

Dr. Michael Bohan – Thank you mentor Mike
St George Lee – editing, advise, and quotes from your book
Fritz – editing and good conversation
To Lee E. for your meditations

To my longtime friends in the sexual recovery groups I attend and to my new friends I have met during the writing and publishing of this work;

To my Sponsor Cliff who with the aid of my Higher Power helped save my life from addiction to sex; and my friend Mike B who pushed me in the right direction; to David Knox for his inspiration;

To my Sponsees who patiently allowed me to sponsor them through the 12 Steps of recovery using this workbook the last four years and who have taught me more about recovery than I could ever give back to them;

To my Higher Power who never gives up on me and who honored my simple prayer of help.

———————————————————

PREFACE

In the beginning of recovery from sexual addiction I was not always willing to give up my sex habits (addiction) entirely. I wanted to but total abstinence from all of my bottom line – addictive behaviors was out of the question.

I attended a few sexual recovery meetings beginning in 1987 . Some years later I went to at least three meetings a week. I still continually acted out on one or more of my undesirable sexual behaviors weekly or sometimes daily. I didn't know what was wrong. I couldn't stay abstinent (sexually sober) from all of my unhealthy behaviors. Just attending meetings was not enough.

What was wrong with my recovery plan was that I had no recovery plan. I was trying to get sober using my own thinking.. My own best thinking got me to where I was – hopeless and a life unmanageable by me. I needed a Sponsor who had worked the 12 Steps of Recovery with a Sponsor himself.

I found a Sponsor who helped me work through the 12 Steps developed by AA but that he adapted for recovery form sexual addiction. My life began to change through this process that took about 15 months to complete meeting one hour a week. Thank you Cliff. In getting sober I began sponsoring others using similar techniques my Sponsor employed. I made notes as I sponsored others recovering form this addiction and wrote The Circle Of Life workbook series for sex addicts and a workbook for alcoholics.

Answering the questions in this workbook are meant to cause a sex addict to ponder their compulsive thoughts and addictive behaviors and begin working the steps with a sponsor utilizing this book with its main goal of sexual sobriety.

INTRODUCTION

The Circle Of Life workbook deals with sexual addiction where we discuss and work through the 12 Step recovery process.

Sex addiction is a disease of the body, mind, and spirit. This is the experience of many of us who are in recovery from sexual addiction, our strength is the result of being sponsored through the 12 Steps, and our hope is in recovery from this addiction by emulating the success of those who have gone before us. Those seasoned in recovery.

The Circle Of Life was developed to help with the basics of recovery. A strong emphasis is placed on obtaining and utilizing a 12 Step program sponsor (note: counselors are recommended for life problems whereas sponsors take us through the 12 Steps of recovery). We stress attendance of sexual addiction support meetings and developing a support system. The intention of this workbook is to *aid* recovering sex addicts in working through the 12 Steps with a sponsor. This workbook does not address formal religion or dogma. This process of recovery, we believe through our own experience, is spiritual in nature and *change* through guidance of a Power greater than ourselves becomes the key to recovery.

The first three chapters give information on our addiction, seeking help for recovery from sex addiction, the feelings that are associated with coming into sexual sobriety, and withdrawal from active sexual compulsive behavior. Chapters four through twelve are dedicated to working the 12 Steps.

Chapter one gives information about our sexual disease. It gives examples of compulsive sexual behaviors, of obsessive thoughts accompanied by compulsive behavior leading to sexual acting out. The second chapter is a guide for attending meetings, overcoming stressors in sobriety, getting a sponsor, and using the slogans of our program to keep us stable in early recovery. In chapter three we look at a list of feelings and we try to identify these feelings that have been suppressed by our disease of compulsively acting out. There are scales to measure feelings and tools to manage feelings in this section. We present tools to cope with withdrawal from sex.

As suggested relaxation techniques, there are serenity breaks throughout this book,as well as program checklists to measure our progress in sobriety.

The remaining chapters are dedicated to working through steps 1 through 12 for sexual recovery with a sponsor. After working the 12 Steps, we continue using them as a tool to stay abstinent from our compulsive sexual behaviors and we sponsor others. Our goal is to internalize the steps and use them daily.

It is possible to recover from sex addiction. Recovery is possible if one has the capacity or develops the capacity to be honest – honest with themselves and honest with their recovering friends.

By utilizing the tools and by working the 12 Steps in this workbook with a sponsor, we believe that it is possible to get and stay sober from compulsive sexual behaviors. By applying the steps we have worked, and by practicing these principles in our life on a daily basis, an abundant life is available to us.

There are probably many ways to work the 12 Steps. As sex addicts, we need people who understand our problem with sex and have a proven way out of an addictive lifestyle. This workbook was developed as an *aid* to recovering people who seek guidance from other recovering sex addicts.

What about the other 12 Step programs not associated with recovery from sexual addiction? Won't they work for our sexual addiction? Do I have to work the steps again? A man in recovery first from alcoholism and then from sexual addiction reports that he initially thought that his recovery work from alcohol would take care of his sexual recovery. He later discovered that he could not recover from his sexual addiction without working the 12 Steps and attending meetings specifically aimed at his sexual addiction. Some of his alcohol recovery literature mentioned help for sexual problems but made no reference to specific help for sexual addiction. He said, "I had the concept of sex problems confused with sexual addiction." I now know that I have an addiction to sex like I had an addiction to alcohol and the alcohol recovery program helped me with my alcohol addiction. I have great loyalty to that program, and I am eternally grateful for it but I now know that I have to go to programs that are specific for sexual addiction recovery. Taking responsibility for my sexual addiction is part of my seventh step in my alcohol recovery program where I humbly asked God to remove my character defects".

The proceeding paragraph is directed towards people who are in other 12 Step programs and who are loyal to a particular 12 Step program and who may not seek or accept help for their compulsive sexual behavior and addiction because of that loyalty. If you have been in other 12 Step programs we suggest you approach this work as if you are a newcomer. Take your time and ponder each question in this workbook. If this is unclear for you – go to a sexual recovery meeting and talk about it. Get a temporary sponsor you can bounce things off of.

This book has no affiliation with any 12 Step program. It does use the 12 Step alcohol recovery program concept simply oriented more toward recovery from sexual addiction. Twelve Step groups are antonymous and have no connection/affiliation with outside entities. This book was developed *by* recovering sex addicts *for* sex addicts who attend one or more 12 Step recovery groups for sex addiction.

The name of the workbook title *The Circle of Life* is derived from the children's movie *The Lion King* and the circle concept is described by Full Spectrum Recovery & Counseling Services at: http://fullspectrumrecovery.com and adapted for this workbook as: the addiction circle, the ritual circle and the growth area. Writing this book is an example of a *growth area* behavior for me and it evolved day by day. The growth area is known here as The Circle Of Life: *where we want to get to - where we want to live.*

Our hope is that *The Circle Of Life* will help you get and stay sober. There is no cure for sexual addiction: Once an addict always an addict. As one recovering person said, "Once a pickle, always a pickle; you can't turn back into a cucumber." The 12 Step process helps to arrest this disease of sexual addiction– to cause it to go into a slumber and in effect stop causing chaos in our lives. As some groups say while holding hands at the end of meetings "Keep Coming Back, it works when you work it and work it cause you're worth it."

You are commended on your courage in simply looking at this problem. The key is to stay honest with yourself, keep an open mind toward the input of others, and be willing to go to any length to change in working through the steps– *honest, open minded, and willing.*

In this workbook we have provided spaces to write your answers and the book offers plenty of space in the margins to jot notes and references if needed. We used larger font sizes as well so that it makes for an easier read.

At the end of this book we will ask anyone who is interested in sharing their personal stories with us to describe what happened as they established a program of recovery from sex addiction after working the 12 Steps presented in this workbook. We would like to know what happened in your lives before and after beginning recovery. We will provide an address that you may send your stories to. Keep in mind that we reserve the right to edit these articles you send and that the stories become the sole property of KJ NIVIN Circle Publications. Anonymity will be observed. Please send all stories typed, double spaced, and please write the stories in English for all who wish to participate. Your story may be included in a future publication.

Visit our website/blog at: https://sites.google.com/site/circleoflifesite/
http://kjnivin-circleoflife.blogspot.com/

(NOTE: Be sure to keep all journals and this workbook in a private place. Privacy is important).

The Serenity Prayer

God Grant Me The Serenity

To Accept

The Things I Cannot Change

The Courage

To Change The Things I Can

And The Wisdom

To Know The Difference

By: Reinhold Niebuhr

PART 1: INTRO TO SEXUAL ADDICTION

SEXUAL ADDICTION

CHAPTER 1

SEXUAL ADDICTION

A Closer Look

The Problem: Our sexual addiction is cunning, baffling, and powerful. It is cunning because it slips up on us and without thinking we are back to acting out again. Baffling because after we are caught up in our addictive behaviors again, we are baffled at how our addiction has us in its grips once more. Powerful because when we attempt to gain control over our addictive behavior and stop our acting out, it seems to get worse. We are out of control again and shame, guilt, and remorse are looming just over the horizon.

Some who don't understand the nature of our sexual addiction (disease) have their own thoughts about what sexual compulsion and addiction is. Some may think that a sex addict awakes in the morning and follow school children to school, in the afternoon they flash others. In the evening, they think, the addict may go to strip clubs and see prostitutes or escorts, then round off their day with window peeping and Internet porn. Contrary to this line of thinking, sex addicts usually have a particular compulsive focus that becomes their primary acting out behavior. Yes it is possible that a sex addict will engage in the all of the above mentioned examples of acting out but that is possibly *the exception and not the rule.*

Most of us engage in only a few major compulsive sexual pursuits. We also may have set rituals that we engage in prior to acting out.

Like other addictions, the disease of sexual addiction is progressive in nature. Even when we stop the actual sexual acting out behaviors, our diseased thought process may be progressing. We can interrupt our acting out thoughts by getting into recovery, but first it is necessary to identify what our disease is. What is the definition of our own particular problem as it relates to uncontrollable sexual addiction? How do we define what are our own compulsive sexual behaviors?

Webster defines *compulsion* as a strong irresistible impulse to perform an act, especially one that is irrational or contrary to one's will. *Addiction* is defined as dependence on or commitment to a habit and cessation from which may cause trauma. Does this sound familiar? To keep it simple, we have a compulsion to sex that is beyond our control. No matter what we want to do we can't stop acting out, and if we do stop we can't stay stopped. We are definitely committed to our acting out behaviors even at the risk of destroying our lives or the lives of others. Stopping our sexual compulsive behavior even for a short time causes emotional and even physical pain. This is the nature of addiction – a sexual addiction; cunning, baffling, powerful.

Many of us admit that we used sex to medicate; to medicate feelings that are negative, to enhance our moods or maybe to use sex as an attempt to gain control of our lives or over others. Some of us may get into a sexual drunken state before or after acting out. Not necessarily a staggering physical drunk but an emotional drunk with emotional hangovers as well. Our egos, whether displayed as low self-esteem or as great self-importance, are usually front and center in our relationships and this seems to push people away or at least keeps them at arms length. We may not experience many feelings other than basic feelings of anger, resentment, fear, lust (which we may mistake for love), happiness, grief, shame, guilt, envy. We preempt any uncomfortable feeling by using sexual *obsession and sexual compulsion* to numb ourselves. When we medicate our feelings through sexual acting out, they become *shadow feelings* or *feelings light* because these feelings are only a ghostly image of what is normal for others.

Our sexual obsession may come in the form of focusing our attention (or a big percentage of it) on acting out possibilities or about past acting out experiences. When obsessing didn't do it for us then the compulsive sexual act itself would stop most uncomfortable feelings until we experienced the feelings of shame and guilt that were generated by acting out. This obsessing and acting out (which triggered compulsion to act out more to try to avoid the guilt we felt) became a vicious cycle (read *Out of The Shadows* by Patrick Carnes Ph.D.). We engaged in this over and over with no hope of ever stopping. Our attempts to *self-medicate* finally turned against us. Trying to medicate our feelings eventually failed to work and the shame caught up with us. The problem is that by the time our acting out had stopped having the effect of medicating our feelings we were hooked. We felt as if we needed to continue to act out just to avoid being depressed.

Compulsive Sexual Behavior

We became hooked on sex and every thought was run through the sexual filter. Our entire life was permeated with sexual addiction. This thread ran through the fabric of our life and touched every facet. Each time these fantasies set off a sensation in our body or mind and

26

we would get a *hit* – a sex hit (like one would expect from getting a marijuana hit). This started our spiral downward into a world of fantasy and lust, and the vicious cycle of sex addiction would rear its ugly head again. We engaged in intrigue: plotted, coerced, planned, and flirted, and nearly always these behaviors culminated into exciting but degrading acts of sex. It degraded us, and those we acted out with when they were exposed to our behavior or when they found out about our problem. Yes, we were certainly hooked – we were sex junkies (Sexaholics Anonymous). Our mental obsession took us to a state of sexual arousal that controlled us.

Answer the following questions and go over them with your sponsor. These discussions will lead to defining your addiction in Step 1:

1) What sexual behaviors do you believe are troublesome to you or others presently?

a) _____

_____

b) _____

_____

c) _____

_____

d) _____

_____

e) _____

_____

f) _____

_____

Using the *a to z list* below, check the categories your compulsive sexual behaviors have fallen under in the present or in the past. Double check the ones you strongly identify with. Go over this list with your sponsor. When we use the two *circles* later in Chapter 4 these behaviors will be entered into the *addictive circle.*

 a. Adult book stores
 b. Anonymous sex (short time knowing partner or partners) or making anonymous phone calls
 c. Bestiality
 d. Bondage (mild or aggressive)
 e. Cross dressing
 f. Escorts / entertainers (buying, selling, trading sex or sexual entertainment)
 g. Exhibitionism – e.g. overt (flashing) or covert (revealing clothing or positioning), walking past window for sexual gratification etc.
 h. Forced or coerced sex (inside or outside a committed relationship), inappropriate touching etc.
 i. Inappropriate consensual sex (with another's husband, wife, significant other etc.
 j. Internet porn or (sex) chat, cams
 k. Making sexual home videos or professional sex movies or being sexual on web cams, sexual text pictures etc.
 l. Masochism
 m. Masturbation (compulsive) with or without fantasy, privately, in an auto, in public, at work etc.)
 n. Molestation (children, an invalid, the impaired etc.)
 o. Nudist facilities and parks
 p. Parties (sexual in nature)
 q. Phone sex (also sexual letters, E-mail, chat etc.)
 r. Pity sex (have sex because of sympathy-those we pity)
 s. Porn video/audio or sexual reading material
 t. Prostitution (buying or selling sex for money or barter)
 u. Self sex with objects or devices
 v. Sex in dangerous places or threat of disease, dangerous sex acts (choking), unprotected sex
 w. Sex in inappropriate places (while driving, in public, at work, in a park etc., with or without a partner)
 x. Strip clubs and establishments (working in or attending)
 y. Violent sexual behavior (with self or with a partner), with objects or devices, stalking, rape etc.

z. Voyeurism e.g. (viewing sexually, window peeping, looking down blouses, into cars, secret filming or pictures, around malls, bathrooms, dressing rooms etc.)

2) Name the most troublesome sexual behavior (s) on the *a to z* list and state why they are a problem (past or present)? (Use bullet comments for most of your answers.)

_____

_____

_____

_____

3) Do you have other sexual behaviors that are less destructive but that are causing difficulty in your life?

_____

_____

_____

_____

4) Do you think you've hit a bottom (all time low) concerning sex? (Yes)   (No) Explain.

_____

_____

_____

5) Do you ever stop a behavior and switch to other sexual behaviors and later go back to that same behavior (e.g. replace window peeping with Internet porn – for a short time)? Explain.

_____

_____

_____

_____

6) Has anyone ever commented or complained about your habits concerning sex - were you embarrassed, did you feel guilt or were you indifferent? Explain what your feelings were.

_____

_____

_____

_____

7) Have you ever switched categories that began to trouble you and replace them *permanently* with another equally compulsive behavior? (This may indicate progression) Name them.

_____

_____

_____

_____

8) If you had to narrow it down to one particular behavior that you gravitate towards most, what would it be (explain)?

_____

_____

_____

_____

These most troublesome sexual behaviors can be considered your *addictive circle* behaviors (sometimes referred to as bottom line behaviors). With your sponsor's help you may come up with more behaviors and in a later chapter you will list these items in your addictive circle. For now we begin to *limit or stop* acting out on our most troublesome behaviors.

Obsessive Thought Patterns and Behavior

Next we look at our obsessive thought patterns and behaviors used in rituals that lead to sexual acting out. Obsession over sex can lead to paralysis, by which we mean an inability to act. When we obsessed over potential sex objects (people made into objects in our minds) or over past acting out fantasies, this stopped us form engaging in other more productive thoughts and from acting on productive behaviors; we became emotionally paralyzed.

An example of obsession is fantasy. Fantasy can come in many different forms: sexual, romantic, violent etc. These fantasies can take on a mind of their own. Some live in a make-believe world where sexual fantasy is king. Sometimes we're not present with our children when they approach us for help or play, our wives during sex or conversation or with other family members, friends, and associates. We aren't even present for ourselves. Sometimes it's so bad near the end, before recovery, that even when we want to think about our life we can't concentrate enough to engage in meaningful self-dialog. This becomes part of a ritual that leads to acting out. Fantasies are usually the first obsession we experience in addiction and the last to go in recovery.

Our rituals began with fantasies and progressed to flirting, making mental notes of possible partners, rain-checking (try to make contacts that may become acting out partners in the future if our present object of attraction falls through), touching, monitoring, following, eavesdropping, and other intrigue. We engage in these rituals that eventually lead to acting out. This addict within needs a bigger hit after a shorter time, and we have to go to another *level* in our ritual. We might do drive-bys (at work, on foot or in an auto), go online and prospect, or call a potential sex partner by phone and find out where they are in their present relationships or use your imagination. The addict within, sooner or later, becomes bored and then we have to take it up a notch. We may go out to bars (If we're recovering alcoholics this may be additionally dangerous). We may invite our wife's friends over or engage them on the phone or by E-mail and get sexual feelings as we flirt with them. As all of this is going on, we may be compulsively masturbating and looking at porn on a nightly and daily basis in the privacy of our home or at work or even in public. The time comes when we act out and then wonder how we got back into it again and why self-restraint didn't help stop us from living this kind of lifestyle. These rituals of obsessive thoughts and behaviors have lead to sexual acting out. They act as *place holders* for our more troublesome acts of compulsive sex. One person in recovery said that if they started to fantasize they would yell out loud: "I'm recovering, I'm not going there today." They related that this gave their addict within notice that they meant business.

9) What obsessive thoughts or behaviors about sex (leading up to acting out) do you believe you have presently?

a) _____

_____

b) _____

_____

c) _____

_____

d) _____

_____

e) _____

_____

f) _____

_____

Using the *a to z list* below, check the categories that your obsessive thoughts and behaviors (leading to acting out) fall under. Double check the ones you strongly identify with. Go over this with your sponsor. When we use the circles later in Chapter 4 these behaviors will be entered into the *ritual circle.*

a. Acting as a people pleaser or needy to attract attention or the possibility of sex, acting helpless or vulnerable
b. Attending church or other organizations to find possible sex partners or love interests
c. Auto gazing (looking into autos for sex hits while driving)

d. Avoiding sex with significant other in order to be sexual with others
e. Constant grooming or preparing (ourselves or others) for sex
f. Constantly listening to romantic or sexually oriented music
g. Cruising for sex or a sex hit (malls, the beach, the street etc.)
h. Doing favors or helping others for attention leading to sex
i. Drive-bys (walking or driving around neighborhood, walking by a person's desk at work, non-aggressive stalking)
j. Eavesdropping (on phone calls, reading personal diaries, on conversations, visual eavesdropping etc.)
k. Fantasizing (about partner, friend, associate or stranger) with or without masturbation
l. Flirting (sexually oriented)
m. Masturbation (the unhealthy variety for us)
n. Monitoring, (following, watching etc.) Keeping tabs
o. Planning sexual encounters
p. Praying for a partner with the potential outcome of having sex
q. Rain-checking (engaging perspective sex partners)
r. Romantic journaling or reading romantic stories for sexual hits
s. Searching dating services for a perspective sex partner or love interest (using phone, computer, newspaper etc.)
t. Smiling or gesturing to entice
u. Spending money to be noticed or to lure others into acting out
v. Staying in unhealthy relationships for the possibility of having sex
w. Suggestive clothing or positioning for sexual gratification
x. Suggestive sexual jokes or conversation
y. Touching (by handshaking, brushing up against others, sexual hugs etc.)
z. TV sex hits (also constant channel changing to get hits), the Internet, web cam, or video sex hits

10) Name the most troublesome sexual obsessive thoughts or behaviors (leading to sexually acting out) from the list above and why these are problems?

_____

_____

_____

_____

11) Do you have other sexual obsessive thoughts or behaviors (not on list) that are less bothersome but cause difficulty in your life and may lead to acting out sexually? Use bullet comments.

_____

_____

_____

_____

12) Do you think you've hit a bottom (all time low) concerning these behaviors? (Yes) (No) Explain.

_____

_____

_____

_____

13) Do you ever stop troublesome obsessive thoughts or behaviors and switch to others (e.g. replace rain checking with fantasy and masturbation)?

_____

_____

_____

_____

14) Has anyone ever commented or complained about your habits concerning obsession (not being alert or not being emotionally or mentally present)? Were you embarrassed or did you feel guilt; what did you feel?

34

_____

_____

_____

_____

_____

15) In what category do you mostly fit into and why (which one category is it that you gravitate towards most)?

_____

_____

_____

_____

The most troublesome of these obsessive thoughts and behaviors can be added to your *ritual* circle in a later chapter (The ritual circle contains slippery thoughts or activities that may motivate you to act out on your addictive behaviors). Remember that the ritual circle is used as a warning tool that tells us as recovering sex addicts that we are engaging in thinking patterns or conduct that will end in a compulsive sexual act (our addiction).

A word about masturbation: There is sometimes confusion concerning appropriateness of masturbation. For some, masturbation is a compulsive problem and for some, it presents no problem. It is possible we may need to abstain from this behavior for a period of time and gradually reintroduce it back into our sexual lives using healthy boundaries. Many therapists suggest a 90 day celibacy period of no sex, including masturbation, early in recovery. If masturbation is not a problem, then it shouldn't be hard to stop for 90 days. We may want to eliminate *fantasy* from our masturbation and replace it with healthy loving thoughts. A man in a recovery meeting once suggested that masturbation could have different levels where we start off with only good intentions, thinking about our spouse or our significant other during masturbation but, eventually, we substitute the healthy loving thoughts for lustful mental contemplation. Eventually this process may evolve into fantasy about others with no thought of being in a committed relationship. We basically masturbate to mental porn. (Thank you Steve S.). These practices may lead to acting out sexually.

Masturbation may go into our *ritual* or eventually, possibly our *growth area*. If it tends toward being compulsive, however, then we probably want to place it in our *addictive circle* and attempt to abstain from it one day at a time (See Ch. 4). We share our concerns with our support group and our sponsor, but ultimately we are the ones who have to decide whether masturbation can be placed on our menu of healthy sexual behaviors.

The next exercise is called *The Serenity Break*. Many recovering people use stress relief or relaxation methods to calm themselves or to simply relax for a few moments. By using this technique, as simple as it looks, we can alter our mood if practiced on a regular basis. This calming practice will help us later on in the 11th Step when we begin practicing prayer and meditation. Some will want to skip this vital tool but the simple things in recovery are sometimes the most important. Please practice taking a Serenity Break.

Take a 15 second serenity break

Rest for a few moments……relax…

Take a deep breath, hold a few seconds (not more than three seconds) and let it all out completely and relax…… let go.
Allow your body to relax; …your legs, …your stomach, …your jaw, chest and back … shoulders … arms …neck …face..eyes.

Now see how that feels. If you participated in this exercise – great!

Use this technique during a stressful time and monitor your body as you practice this. You may be lying down, sitting, standing, or even walking,
Focus on being calm and let your mind relax. Calm – be still and just be.

Daily Sobriety Plan

It is wise to make a daily sobriety plan. A few minutes of meditating, thinking about the day ahead, will allow you to plan your day so there isn't dead time. It is OK to relax during the day and not just work constantly. Relaxation can be structured into the sobriety plan but, be aware that, the addict within seems to thrive during boredom or unstructured time. What is a sobriety plan?

When we awaken we do our normal things to prepare ourselves for the day. As we go through our normal routine we think of the day ahead. We might consider this: Am I working a full day; if not then what? I picture myself getting home or running errands and the approximate time of day. I allow time to eat and change clothes. Is there a meeting tonight? If not, plan on calling someone or if there is a meeting, make a mental note of the time to leave home and picture arriving at the meeting. This may help you not be diverted into cruising while driving to a recovery meeting. If you go out after the meeting, factor that in. Consider what time you will get back home. If there is no meeting for that night, make a call and then plan what is next. Maybe study this workbook or read sexual recovery literature or other recovery/spiritual material. In early sobriety it is necessary to have a plan each day. Later you may be able to look through the entire week and plan your sober walk. Remember that balance of family, work, alone time, recovery work, and other parts of your life is most important in maintaining sobriety. We make plans but *we don't plan the outcome.*

The sobriety plan can be written or mental notes made as long as there is a daily plan. Keep it as simple as possible but in early recovery it is best to write it out. This daily plan may keep us from mentally straying back into that old familiar groove of compulsive sex. Here is an example of a plan:

Wake up 6:00 AM
Do prayer / meditation reading
Eat and get ready (walk dog)
Work at 9:00 AM
Noon Lunch at home with husband
Get off work 4:00 PM (walk dog)
Eat and relax until 6:30 PM
Meeting at 7:00 PM until 8:30 PM
Home at 9:00 PM – journal about my day
Relax until 9:30 PM – Make a call to recovering member or sponsor
Read sexual recovery material and do workbook until 10:15 PM
Pray and think about my day. Mentally tab pluses and minuses but don't dwell on them
Bed 10:45 PM

Try to stick to the plan but not rigidly. As long as we know basically what our day may look like and as long as we are covered by a plan of sobriety to avoid unstructured time, we can stay in a recovery mode.

Another day might look like this:
Wake up 6:00 AM
Do prayer / meditation reading
Work at 9:00 AM
Noon Lunch with friends
Get off work 5:00 PM
Eat and relax until 6:30 PM
Run errands and such until 8:00 PM
Home at 8:30 PM - journal about my day
Relax and maybe do a hobby until 10:00 PM – Make a call to a recovering member or sponsor
Read some spiritual material
Pray and think about my day.
Bed 11:00 PM

Look closely at free time (weekends and days off). Some who are retired may need to add structure into their lives. Here is a weekend scenario:

Saturday

Wake up at 8:00 AM
Eat and get ready / pray, meditate - (10 minutes)
Go shopping with wife - go to a 10:30 recovery meeting
Get home at Noon
Do some chores, projects, play tennis with spouse, kids soccer game etc.
(If I have something irritating me I make a *bookend* call by calling someone about a problem and later when it is dealt with call them again to talk about how you've handled the problem)
Schedule some relaxation time or a nap in the afternoon 2:30 PM
Eat and shower 4:30 PM
Meet with my sponsor at 6 PM to read recovery literature and go over my workbook.
Get home at 7:30 PM
Talk with significant other and maybe go out to eat

Sunday

Up at 9 AM
Pray and meditate – (25 minutes)
Go for jog and get prepared to go to church
Church 11 AM
Go for family canoe ride 1 to 3 PM
Visit friend in hospital 4 to 5 PM

Alone time: watch a TV program, read a novel/recovery material, call parents/relatives, go to a movie etc.

Eventually we develop a new pattern of recovery and a life of value. It may be beneficial to write your sobriety plan down for the next week just to see what it looks like. Use the example below to develop a sobriety plan.

Be sure to include your *sobriety actions* (journaling, prayer, relaxation practices, meetings etc.) in your daily sobriety plan. You may want to write this out now or wait until you are starting your day. The sobriety plan may be used to bring about more balance in your sober walk.

Day One	Day Two

In this chapter we have learned about our addiction and about a daily sobriety plan. We have digested much to help us along the path of growth. Our next growth area is about *getting started* in the recovery process in Chapter 2.

GETTING STARTED

`

CHAPTER 2

GETTING STARTED

The Process of Recovery

Recovery is a process and not an event. A process takes time to complete and an event is something that happens instantly or very quickly. Recovery doesn't happen quickly as a recovering friend Mike C. says: "I wanted to work a step a week and that was the pace I wanted to start out with but my sponsor informed me that working the 12 Steps takes time, something not to be rushed. It eventually took us over a year, meeting weekly, to work through the steps - a pace I now use with my responses. "

In the beginning of recovery we need to first admit that we have a problem, find a recovery program, attend meetings, listen, and share and above all obtain a sponsor. Two books many read in early recovery are *Out of The Shadows* by Patrick Carnes, a basic description of sex addiction and its many aspects, and a daily meditation book called *Answers in the Heart* by P. Williamson and S. Kiser. The important thing here is to find out about our disease. These books help give us perspective on our dilemma. You may be very confused in the beginning and not be able to figure out what is compulsive and what isn't. The bottom line is that we have been compulsive towards sex and eventually have become addicted to it. We need to address it before it ruins our life.

A word about abstinence and celibacy: A recovering sex addict related the following: "Someone in my first meetings told me to consider abstinence from my compulsive sexual behavior and to even consider celibacy from all sex....say for ninety days: What an order, I can't go through with it – was my first thought. How could I stop all sex and live. After thinking about it for a while and remembering how bad it was in the past, I decided to go for it. I bravely white knuckled it for 90 days. I began to see my "Addict" within and experience its control over me. I experienced severe physical withdrawal, and I felt crazy in the beginning of the 90 days of celibacy." We are neither for nor against celibacy for long durations here. However, it is this author's belief that it is beneficial to stop all sexual behavior for a period of time defined and agreed upon with your sponsor and agreed upon with your significant other if you are in a "committed" non-addictive relationship. After that agreed upon period of time is over, we still abstain from our addictive sexual behaviors or behaviors that lead to addiction that were troublesome to ourselves and to others. (*NOTE: T*he term *celibacy* here refers to abstaining from all sex. The term *abstinence* means abstaining from our compulsive sexual behaviors but still participating in healthy sex as defined later in our two circles in the 1st Step).

Seeking Help

We now embark on a journey of more action. You went into action when you obtained this workbook. Now it is time for action and more action. This is an action program. We change our priorities to accommodate recovery and make ample time for it so we don't *slip* back into addiction.

A *slip* refers to acting out on one or more of our addictive sexual behaviors and the acronym S.L.I.P. stands for *sobriety lost its priority.* So remember that sobriety is the priority.

Early on in our recovery we go to as many sexual addiction recovery meetings as our schedule will permit. It is wise to go to at least a meeting or two a week if possible. Online meetings are available for those who can not easily make local meetings. Counselors may have helpful groups as well. You may have to travel a distance to attend a meeting. One member had to travel eighty miles one way for the first six months of his recovery. We go to any length to get and stay sexually sober. If there are no meetings nearby, eventually you may want to start a meeting in your area (refer to Appendix III for resources). I find that a book by Bruce Brown called *Understanding12 Step Programs (A Quick Reference Guide)* is a great source that explains 12 Step Programs in general and may help give perspective on attending meetings.

Throughout this workbook you will find questions and spaces for answering the questions. Please answer the questions using the lines provided and explain each answer (in most cases not with only a *Yes* or *No* answer). This process of answering the questions thoroughly helps to promote understanding of your addictive nature. Make note of actions you are suggested to perform on a regular basis as a reminder to complete the task (i.e. journaling, stressor list, obtain phone numbers, find sponsor, etc.)

Ask yourself these questions:

1) Admitting that we have compulsive sexual behaviors is necessary to begin our recovery. Have I surrendered to the idea that my sexual behaviors may be causing me or others problems or difficulty? Explain.

_____

_____

_____

_____

2) Do I feel comfortable or at least OK about being in a sexual recovery meeting or seeking help from recovering people? Explain.

_____

_____

_____

_____

_____

_____

_____

_____

3) Are the meetings or recovery support helpful to me? Name two ways they are helpful.

_____

_____

_____

_____

4) The only requirement for membership of 12 Step sexual recovery meetings is a *desire* to stop our addictive and/or compulsive sexual behavior. Do I have a desire to stop a particular sexual behavior (or more than one)? List them.

_____

_____

_____

_____

o Accepting responsibility for our compulsive sexual disease and behaviors is something of a daunting task. We first have to admit that we have a problem and then we must accept the fact that we need to do something about this potentially fatal disease each day. We also need the help of our Higher Power and others.

5) Do I have a problem with the concept of a Higher Power – God as you choose to understand God? Explain.

_____

_____

_____

_____

o If you do have a problem with the concept of a Higher Power, consider using the recovery group as a power greater than yourself. Remember, there is no requirement to believe anything. The steps and concepts are meant to be suggestive only. (Of course it is suggested as well that if you parachute from an airplane that you pull the rip cord in order to inflate the parachute.)

_____

6) Am I still holding on to any old ideas that would cause me not to reach out and ask for help? For example: Men don't ask for help; I feel too vulnerable as a female among these

recovering men. Name any reservations that may hold you back from seeking help from others.

_____

_____

_____

_____

7) Sharing in meetings may be difficult; we've lived a lifetime of secrecy; we've lived double lives. Begin slowly. Pull someone aside if necessary to talk with (be sure there isn't sexual attraction on your part towards this person). Do I have problems sharing in meetings or with others about my addiction?

_____

_____

_____

_____

○ There are two basic types of meetings you may attend–*Closed and Open*. To attend a closed meeting you will likely be required to admit that you have a desire to stop acting out sexually in order to attend the meeting by stating the type of compulsive sexual behavior you wish to stop. An open meeting is for those who wish to find out information about sexual addiction; attendees are not asked to qualify. Find a meeting nearby or online as a part of your recovery process. This may take some effort. Don't give up. Persistence pays off. Use the resources around you and begin attending meetings as soon as possible (ASAP).

A word about *trust:* Most of us sex addicts have lived a double life of secrecy and fear. This form of isolation has to be eliminated as we share our problems in our support groups. Most meetings offer a safe place to unload our burdens about our compulsive sexual behaviors. A used car salesman said this to me once after I made a big deal about signing some papers to purchase a car "You are going to have to trust someone – sometime" and he was right. I have to trust enough to share in my group and to others the exact nature of my sex problems. We develop trust as we go through the process of recovery. In some instances we may want to talk to another group member in private about our addictive behavior and be sure to ask that what you say will be kept confidential.

Stressors

There are many stressors in our lives and these stressors seem to get pushed to the back as newer more pressing problems arise. Here are some examples written in bullet format:

Need oil change in car/tires are worn
Grass needs mowing
Scuffed new shoes
Laundry needs attending to
Pet needs to go to the vet
Neighbor bugging me to give back his tools again
Stressed about children's grades/little time to help them
Bank account overdrawn/family spending too much
Worried about job, boss was angry at me yesterday
Co-workers resent my sexual jokes
Wife found out about my acting out with porn
I acted out last night
(list more)

8) List your stressors from the least to the greatest or in any order as they come to mind, you may be surprised how many come up. Be specific.

_____

_____

_____

_____

_____

_____

_____

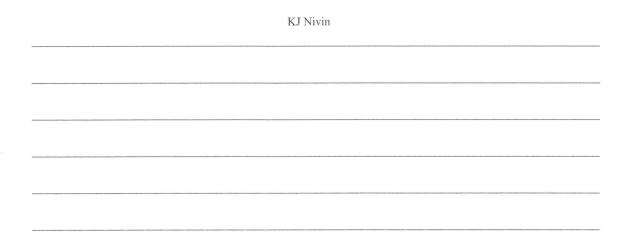

○ Use this technique of identifying stressors on a weekly basis while working the first three steps and as a tool throughout recovery. This is not a *to do* list, it is a purge list. We are only interested in identifying stressors. After making the list, place it where you can see it weekly and notice how many of the stressors begin to fall off the list as we focus on working the steps. The point of this exercise is to get it out of our heads and onto paper (we dump it).

This tool helps stimulate our thinking process and puts us in touch with our hidden stress. Don't shortcut yourself; write until you feel as though you've run out of things to write. Be sure to include minor worries, frets, fears and resentments towards others as well. It is not unusual to end up with fifteen to thirty entries. This is part of journaling, try this weekly.

Good Orderly Direction

A sponsor is a person who will help a newly recovering sex addict work the 12 Steps. They are not counselors or clergy. They are people who have gone through the process of recovery and who continue this process by sponsoring others. Use this section as preparation for obtaining a sponsor. Finding a sponsor is a process and may take time but don't put it off too long. This may be one of the biggest decisions you make in your life. If you have a sponsor, discuss sponsorship expectations with him or her in depth. Alternatively, you may use a group member or someone in recovery from sex addiction as a temporary sponsor.

The most important decision in recovery is to decide that we can't do this alone. We need guidance from someone who is successfully staying sexually sober. We should have no sexual attraction to this person so as not to be distracted while working through this life-saving process.

Many are ashamed of their sexual past. Others don't realize that their best thinking got them to this desperate point in their lives. For either reason, they may not seek another's help.

As newcomers to recovery we need to swallow our pride and begin our search for an appropriate person to sponsor us through the 12 Steps.

> *Assignment:* **Take the steps necessary to find a sexual recovery meeting and also ask a person to sponsor you. To find a sponsor, go to several meetings and then ask someone who might seem appropriate for you. Ask to meet with your perspective sponsor so that you might get to know them better. Ask if they have worked through the 12 Steps with a sponsor themselves. Once you have decided on a sponsor, set up a regular time to meet with them in person or by other means of communications (E-mail, phone, text messaging etc.) When you first meet with your sponsor write a stressor list for the week and go over it.**

Answer the questions in this workbook to the best of your ability. Review each one with your sponsor. (Suggestion: Meet with your sponsor approximately one hour a week dedicated to working on this recovery process. Do your homework during the week prior to meeting with your sponsor).

9) Who is your sponsor? Write the name and date here.

_____

o If you have any difficulty finding an appropriate sponsor then ask someone to be a temporary sponsor or ask if you can just call them. (If they are unable to sponsor you, they may know of someone who can.) Find out their schedule so you will know when they are available to contact. Some may not be available to sponsor you. Don't take it personally. You will find the appropriate person. It just takes persistence.

10) What sexual addiction recovery group do you find most helpful?

_____

o You may want to consider this your home group and attend it on a regular basis.

11) In the next few weeks obtain at least three other contacts besides your sponsor (people you aren't attracted to) and call at least two of them weekly. List their first names and phone numbers here. It may take several tries to reach them. As we progress we obtain more names and numbers. (Your support group may have a member phone list.)

_____

_____

_____

_____

12) Did you obtain a copy of *Answers in the Heart* by Hazelden (meditation book for sex addicts) and *Out of the Shadows* by Patrick Carnes? Yes   No   (if not, why not)

o Begin reading the meditation book each morning and study sexual addiction recovery material on a regular basis. The meditation will start you thinking about recovery early in your day and sexual recovery literature will give information concerning this addiction. Your recovery group may have recovery literature.

13) Journaling is worthwhile to add to our daily recovery program. We write down our thoughts and behaviors in a private journal so that our thoughts have another outlet. In time we can also review our journal and look at our progress. *Do I have a private place to store a journal* and note my progress and some of my recovery issues? (You may want to consider your privacy concerning anything you write about your addiction including this workbook.) Yes   No

o Begin journaling daily and take care to place it where you can maintain privacy.

More Tools

This is a program of action and the above actions are necessary to develop new recovery tools. We can't think our way into sober living; we must live our way into sober thinking. Each action we take on a regular basis helps us to get the proper information into our thinking process and this will eventually take the place of our old thinking patterns. We "*re-program*" our thinking by practicing actions on a daily basis. The saying "practice makes perfect" applies here although we must remember that we are striving for *progress not perfection*. We work our program today and live by the slogan *one day at a time* or even one moment at a time to stay sexually sober. The recovery actions we do daily make up our program.

Here are some slogans that many in recovery use to put things into perspective when thrown off balance by a situation or events. Just like the parachute mentioned previously, these are only suggestions.

USE THESE SLOGANS FOR BALANCE

ONE MOMENT AT A TIME

FIRST THINGS FIRST

IF IT WORKS DON'T FIX IT

BUT FOR THE GRACE OF GOD THERE GO I

H.A.L.T. (Hungry, Angry, Lonely, Tired)

More slogans:

HONESTY IS THE POLICY

EASY DOES IT

LIVE AND LET LIVE

PROGRESS NOT PERFECTION

ONE DAY AT A TIME

UTILIZE (Don't Analyze Utilize)

THINK THINK THINK

These short phrases, or slogans, may be used in a stressful time to interrupt our thinking long enough to regain mental composure and avoid negative or sexual thought processes. Write these down in a place where you can see them – on your bathroom mirror, a desk you use often or anywhere else you can see them privately and read them daily. These phrases may seem silly, but they can be powerful when used in the framework of sobriety. We may want to repeat these slogans to ourselves if we become stressed or we may want to consider the spirit of the phrase in order to redirect our thoughts or actions.

The slogan *Easy Does It* is among the slogans found in the AA Big Book of Alcoholics Anonymous as are other slogans. It can be used in moments of anger or frustration to remind us to slow down, (Rome or Rome.com) wasn't built in a day. Take it easy and *Think, Think, Think.* Think before acting out over stressful situations. Stress will be present. It is up to us to handle stress in an appropriate, non-addictive manner.

Live and Let Live can be used to keep from judging others or being resentful towards them. We try to allow them to move on and we practice cleaning off our own side of the street and finding out what is going on inside us. There is a saying in the rooms: "If I'm not the problem, there is no solution." We may not be the problem but if we have a problem then it effects us. We look at what is upsetting us and correct that.

One Day At A Time or *One Moment At A Time* is used to help prevent us from projecting negativity into the future or from worrying about our past (Which after all can't be changes!). This may keep us far away from focusing on the things at hand in the present day. We are not promised tomorrow. What can I do today to prepare for tomorrow or straighten out the mess I may have made in the past? (It is explained later in this workbook that the tools of the program and the 12 Steps are used for this purpose.) At times we may be triggered by a person in our presence or by a fantasy. If so practice "one moment at a time." We may use this tool by practicing the *three second pause.* Here is a description presented by St. George Lee: In the first second, we might catch ourselves objectifying someone or noticing that someone is sexually attractive. In the next second, we turn away and place that person in a positive light. For example, she is someone's sister, daughter, etc. We might also say a quick prayer. In the third second, we observe the person again and bathe them in light as a child of God. In so doing, we practice living in the moment in a healthy way, being present to ourselves and to others. Lastly we turn back to the business at hand and living addiction free.

If It Works Don't Fix It We find out what works for us in *our* program of recovery and attend to that. Some won't agree or understand that we have a sexual addiction and need to attend meetings. Our gut tells us what is right for us and eventually we will begin to rely on that feeling. Try monitoring your gut area when dealing with a dilemma that needs a decision to be made. If practiced, this little tool can be quite instructive.

Don't Analyze Utilize is for those of us that tend to over-scrutinize things. We may focus too much on what caused our addiction and we stay buried in these details. Instead, in our program of recovery, we begin to focus on how we can make the best of it and concentrate on how to live sexually sober. We utilize our new tool set to stay focused on living in the framework of the 12 Steps on a daily basis.

Progress not perfection helps to gain perspective on working the program and acknowledging our progress instead of berating ourselves for not doing it perfectly. We claim spiritual progress not perfection.

Honesty is the best policy may be thought of as self-honesty. If we are honest with ourselves, we stand a better chance of being honest with others.

H.A.L.T. is an acronym for Hungry, Angry, Lonely and Tired. Some add an S. at the end of HALT to represent S*tressed*. When two or more of these enter into our day, we are in danger of a S.L.I.P. (sobriety lost its priority) so we attend to these problems. If we are hungry we eat something. If angry or lonely we may call another recovering person or go to a meeting. If we are tired we make it a point to rest physically and mentally. If we are stressed we may write a stressor list and discuss it with our sponsor.

There are other slogans that we may learn from meetings or recovering people. We use the slogans as tools to keep us balanced while we are working the 12 Steps and integrating the steps into our life. Eventually these slogans may become a part of our thinking and an automatic response to stress. This automatic response eventually may replace our compulsive behavior.

At this time take a 30 second Serenity Break

---

30 second serenity break

Rest for a few moments…..and relax…you may choose to close your eyes if appropriate.

Take a deep breath, hold for a few seconds and let it out completely and relax……

Allow your body to relax; …your legs, …your stomach, …your jaw, chest and back, … shoulders, … arms, …neck, …face…eyes.

Now let your mind relax. Calm – be still and just be.

Repeat this if necessary. Now see how that feels. If you participated in this short exercise – write out your feelings (physical or emotional).

_____

_____

_____

Use this technique during a stressful time and monitor your body as you practice it. This exercise may be done lying, sitting or standing. Some members record this short relaxation exercise on tape and play it back to themselves while practicing relaxation.

_____

Next in Chapter 3 we look at our thoughts and feelings.

Process of Sexual Recovery

IT'S AN INSIDE JOB

Process of Sexual Recovery

CHAPTER 3

IT'S AN INSIDE JOB

Feelings / Thoughts

In chapter one and two we scratched the surface of sexual compulsion that leads to sex addiction. We talked some about meetings, getting a sponsor and defining our addiction. We'll go further into the addiction later but there is something that is important early on in recovery: The thawing out process. I like to call it *THE BIG THAW*. Our emotions have been frozen or at least not active. When we begin to *not* act out on our addictive circle behaviors on a daily basis, our feelings begin to show themselves. Sometimes they show up in extreme ways. Our likes and dislikes, that may have been stifled in the past, begin to surface. *"Surface"* is an interesting term because to surface means that the feelings would have to have been submerged. The healing of our thought process while beginning to experience our true feelings is an integral part of the recovery process. Recovery is an inside affair. Fix the insides and the outsides seem to take care of themselves.

Feelings tend to influence thoughts and vice versa. As a recovering person from sex addiction, especially early on, we may experience mood swings for the first thirty days or so. Every facet of our being has been touched by addiction. It stands to reason that there is a lot that needs healing, and this takes time. Our thoughts may also be jumbled. Coming off the powerful drug sex (the way an addict uses sex) has similarities to coming off cocaine. Our thinking may be faulty and our memory may also be affected. Our anger and other emotions seem to show up in extreme or inappropriate ways. Let us look at feelings first.

Where do feelings come from? The brain has a little bunch of cells on each side called the amygdale. This part of the brain is shaped like an almond, and "amygdala" is derived from Latin for almond. Scientists believe that the amygdala is the part of the brain that generates emotions. It stores the emotional forms of our memories. So, when we have a sad or happy experience about something the amygdala is working to generate feelings.

One thing we noticed about our feelings in early recovery is that they tended to cause us not to think clearly and we may feel uncomfortable experiencing them. (This will begin to change as we progress in recovery.) In our recovery as former practicing sex addicts, we may have a low opinion of anything associated with feelings. We may even think that people who show feelings are weak. We may pride ourselves for being cool and calm even when others are bouncing off the walls. It may have been that we are numb from the chin up. Coming into sobriety, sex addicts sometimes have difficulty managing these new feelings.

Just what are feelings and how do we manage them? Below is a list of basic feelings that people tend to experience on a normal basis. Remember that "Feelings are not right or wrong; they just are... or that feelings are not facts." The problem lies with where our focus is. Sex addicts tend to focus on negative feelings or false positive ones. We begin to change our focus to more productive thoughts by focusing on our positive feelings and acknowledging our negative ones.

In the destructive and constructive feelings lists below choose (by circling) the feelings that you can identify with. In some cases it may help to use the dictionary for a more clear meaning.

Constructive Feelings

Mild

Alert, amazed, approved, attractive, benevolent, calm, comfortable, content, daring, friendly, graceful, humble, interested, relaxed, sure, smart, smug, untroubled, warm

Moderate

Adventurous, affectionate, amused, appealing, anticipating, curious, determined, esteemed, excited, fond, glad, inspired, intelligent, jolly, liked, mischievous, patient, peaceful, pleased, popular, relieved, yearning

Strong

Appreciated, brave, capable, concerned, consoled, courageous, delighted, eager, enchanted, grateful, gratified, happy, hopeful, infatuated, joyful, optimistic, proud, sympathetic, tender, valiant, vibrant

Intense

Alive, awed, confident, courageous, empathic, enthusiastic, loving, pitying, respected, surprised, zealous, worthy

Destructive Feelings

Mild

Bashful, self-conscious, dependent, discontented, dismal, dismayed, edgy, gloomy, impatient, indifferent, lethargic, listless, mixed-up, moody, puzzled, regretful, reluctant, sullen, tired, timid, upset, unsure

Moderate

Alarmed, annoyed, apathetic, aversive, baffled, defensive, bored, confused, contemptuous, cranky, dejected, disappointed, disdainful, enmity, envious, helpless, inadequate, indecisive, ineffectual, nervous, perplexed, provoked, rancorous, resigned, shy, suspicious, tempted, tense, troubled, uncomfortable, unhappy, weary, worried

Strong

Afraid, antagonistic, anxious, apprehensive, bewildered, bitter, detesting, disgusted, disconnected, dismayed, dissatisfied, disturbed, embarrassed, envious, fatigued, fed-up, forlorn, frustrated, greedy, guilty, hopeless, indignant, inhibited, jealous, mad, rejected, resentful, sad, sick, torn, useless, unconfident, weak, vengeful, worn-out,

Intense

Abandoned, accursed, afraid, angry, cynical, degraded, despised, hateful, estranged, exhausted, furious, futile, horrified, humiliated, hurt, impotent, infuriated, lustful, lonely, miserable, overwhelmed, pained, panicky, rebellious, shameful, scared, shocked, surprised, terrified, threatened, trapped, unloved, worthless.

Overwhelming you say – I agree. There are probably many more words that describe feelings as well. (If you are interested, see http://www. addictionz.com/feelings and emotions.htm for more descriptions of feelings.) If you identified with the negative feelings more than the positive, begin looking each day for positive feelings and identify them. Many addicts quickly see the bad in themselves but have trouble seeing the good. Sometimes our focus is on the negative and our focus can be changed.

Some of us may be able only to identify general feelings like the feelings of fear, anger, frustration, guilt, shame, love, hate, jealousy, envy, happiness, joy, resentment, excitement or confusion. Some may identify more than this; some less. If possible, go beyond these familiar feelings and make note of the more vague feelings as well. It is possible that you are not yet feeling many feelings and still numb somewhat. If this is the case, the feelings will emerge as you are abstinent from compulsive sexual behavior.

Our feelings will become more balanced as time passes. Some of us consult professionals for more information on feelings one might and might not expect. If our feelings remain out of balance, it stands to reason that our thinking process will be affected and we are in danger of acting out if we don't seek help from a professional or a sponsor (or both).

Feelings Exercise

Next let us look at constructive feelings first. Use the scales below to measure your feelings. On a scale of one to ten, circle the number representing how you believe you are affected by the following feelings (one being mild and ten being intense):

Loving – A form of caring

1____2____3____4____5____6____7____8____9____10

Courageous - A form of confidence, faith

1____2____3____4____5____6____7____8____9____10

Joyous - A form of happiness

1____2____3____4____5____6____7____8____9____10

Grateful - A form of respect, thankfulness

1____2____3____4____5____6____7____8____9____10

Calmness- A form of peace

1____2____3____4____5____6____7____8____9____10

Proud (positive) - A form of confidence, self-assurance, good self-image

1____2____3____4____5____6____7____8____9____10

Friendly - A form of kindness, goodness

1____2____3____4____5____6____7____8____9____10

Patience - A form of peace

1____2____3____4____5____6____7____8____9____10

Serene - A form of calmness

1____2____3____4____5____6____7____8____9____10

Sympathetic - A form of caring

1____2____3____4____5____6____7____8____9____10

Confident - A form of self-assuredness, faith

1____2____3____4____5____6____7____8____9____10

Excited - A form of joy, happiness

1____2____3____4____5____6____7____8____9____10

Alive - A form of being excited, confident, joyful

1____2____3____4____5____6____7____8____9____10

Affectionate - A form of love, respect

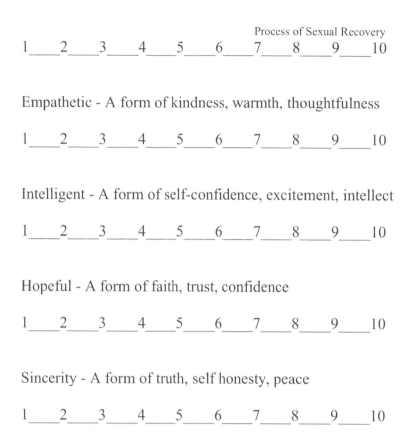

Process of Sexual Recovery

1____2____3____4____5____6____7____8____9____10

Empathetic - A form of kindness, warmth, thoughtfulness

1____2____3____4____5____6____7____8____9____10

Intelligent - A form of self-confidence, excitement, intellect

1____2____3____4____5____6____7____8____9____10

Hopeful - A form of faith, trust, confidence

1____2____3____4____5____6____7____8____9____10

Sincerity - A form of truth, self honesty, peace

1____2____3____4____5____6____7____8____9____10

These constructive feelings are available to all of us, but they may be hidden beneath our addiction, our negative self-image, and our negative feelings. As we recover we bring them to the front and experience them more and more. Consider the feelings listed above. The more often we experience them normally (not medicated by our sexual addiction) the closer it brings us to others. We become more vulnerable.

What would it be like to be joyous most of the time or to feel self-assured? The 12 Steps are used to bring us back to our true feelings. They will help us to *feel better*: We will be able to better feel *more happiness, more pain, more confidence, more sadness, more joy,* etc. In other words we will begin to become in touch with our true feelings.

As active sex addicts we may recognize more of the destructive feelings than the constructive ones. When we get into recovery we may start to experience mood swings. We may experience being very happy one moment and then crying the next or we may be angry and anxious, then change to calm and collected later for no apparent reason. Then we may swing back the other way. Eventually our roller-coaster of emotions even out and we gain more balance. The more in depth that we search ourselves, however, the *more that will be revealed.*

Our feelings come out of hiding and they get the chance to see the light of day. We are no longer numb to life and to our emotions. Our new-found feelings motivate us.

Now let's consider our destructive feelings. Are feelings generated by how we think? We believe that when our judgment is impaired (misjudging a situation or event) our thinking starts becoming negative and feelings start to arise that are negative or falsely positive. One member related this: "I remember reading a scathing letter from my soon to be ex-wife and she accused me of my many shortcomings. I reacted badly and complained to a friend in the program that she had *caused me to feel bad*. He told me this "What if she was on the other side of the world saying the same thing about you and you weren't able to read this letter or hear her verbal bashing? How would you think then; how would you feel?" I told him I wouldn't think anything because I couldn't hear or know that she was angry with me. He informed me that what happened to me in this case is that these messages went into my brain and were processed in a negative way. Ultimately, it is up to *me* what I do with these thoughts and how I process them; that I am choosing to feel bad. That made sense. I was blaming her for my choice of focusing on negative feelings. The only time that anything she was saying about me affected me was when my brain took it in and made a big deal about it. That told me that I really did have a choice."

Use the scales below to measure your destructive feelings. On a scale of one to ten, circle the number representing how you believe you are affected negatively with the following feelings (one being mild and ten being intense):

Anger, Hate – A form of control, fear

1____2____3____4____5____6____7____8____9____10

Resentment (anger re-thought) - A form of control, anger

1____2____3____4____5____6____7____8____9____10

Jealousy - A form of control, fear

1____2____3____4____5____6____7____8____9____10

False Pride - A form of ego

1____2____3____4____5____6____7____8____9____10

Lust - A form of control, selfishness and anger

1____2____3____4____5____6____7____8____9____10

Greed - A form of selfishness, fear

1____2____3____4____5____6____7____8____9____10

Gluttony - A form of self-hate, control, self-medication

1____2____3____4____5____6____7____8____9____10

Envy - A form of hatred and greed

1____2____3____4____5____6____7____8____9____10

Fear - A form of lack of faith and projection

1____2____3____4____5____6____7____8____9____10

People Pleasing - A form of fear and control, manipulation

1____2____3____4____5____6____7____8____9____10

Lying – A form of control involving fear of losing what you have or not getting what you want

1____2____3____4____5____6____7____8____9____10

Control - A form of fear and selfishness, self-centeredness
1____2____3____4____5____6____7____8____9____10

Judgmentalism - A form of control, ego, fear, self-centeredness

1____2____3____4____5____6____7____8____9____10

Manipulation - A form of control, lying, fear

1____2____3____4____5____6____7____8____9____10

Self-Pity - A form of self-centeredness, lack of faith, low self-esteem, self-hatred

1____2____3____4____5____6____7____8____9____10

Isolating - A form of fear, self-centeredness, lack of faith

1____2____3____4____5____6____7____8____9____10

Shame - A form of hopelessness and poor ego

1____2____3____4____5____6____7____8____9____10

Excess Guilt - A form of fear dealing with truth

1____2____3____4____5____6____7____8____9____10

Self-centeredness A form of Selfishness, Self-seeking

1____2____3____4____5____6____7____8____9____10

Low Self-Esteem - A form of self-pity, lack of faith, low self-worth

1____2____3____4____5____6____7____8____9____10

Fear of abandonment - A form of unworthiness, fear

1____2____3____4____5____6____7____8____9____10

Caretaking - A form of control, manipulation, lying, and low self-esteem (doing for others what they could and would benefit from doing for themselves).

1____2____3____4____5____6____7____8____9____10

Irritability - A form of anxiety, self pity, anger

1____2____3____4____5____6____7____8____9____10

Approval Seeking- A form of manipulation, fear, low self-esteem, phoniness, people pleasing

1____2____3____4____5____6____7____8____9____10

Sloth - A form of laziness, fear, self-hatred

1____2____3____4____5____6____7____8____9____10

Perfectionism - A form of control, self-hatred, lack of limits, shame acted in

1____2____3____4____5____6____7____8____9____10

Procrastination - A form of laziness, fear, creating chaos

1____2____3____4____5____6____7____8____9____10

Gossip - A form of fear, control, anger

1____2____3____4____5____6____7____8____9____10

Impatience - A form of fear, anxiety

1____2____3____4____5____6____7____8____9____10

Intolerance - A form of self-centeredness and lack of acceptance

1____2____3____4____5____6____7____8____9____10

Compulsive busyness – A form of avoiding, fear, distraction, self-centeredness

1____2____3____4____5____6____7____8____9____10

Descartes said *as I think- therefore I am.* I believe he didn't go far enough in his explanation. Next is an example of how our thinking can generate negative feelings.

If someone calls me a pumpkin I usually won't react, I know that I am not a pumpkin. On the other hand, if someone calls me an idiot, I may react. Why, because somewhere inside I believe that I am possibly stupid or inept. If I react to this name-calling it is because of my past negative programming that doesn't really match today's reality. It isn't caused by anyone outside of me; it is caused by me and my low self-esteem. Throughout my life I developed self-hatred and blamed others for it. Now, in recovery, I have to change my old way of thinking.

We have many different feelings. We have just measured some of our constructive and destructive feelings by using the scales provided. You may add more feelings to this list. Please continue measuring your feelings to see how strong or mild they are. Think about what other feelings make them up; some feelings are made up of several other feelings. Trying to identify our feelings helps us to feel them better. When we identify our feelings we become more comfortable experiencing them as time passes (give time...time). This helps us to not cover them up with sex because they are uncomfortable to us. We begin to thaw out; we begin to recover. We then begin to have choices: *I choose – therefore I am.*

Withdrawal

As we begin our recovery from sexual addiction, we will usually go through a period of *withdrawal.* Withdrawal may take the form of emotional upheaval or even physical symptoms, and our thoughts and feelings may go through a roller-coaster ride. We may be happy one moment and crying for no apparent reason driving in our car the next. Physical and emotional withdrawal can be mild or it can be quite uncomfortable and difficult. Withdrawal from sex sometimes takes place immediately but, on the other hand, it may take weeks to begin. It depends on the individual. Withdrawal doesn't take place fully until we stop all compulsive acting out behavior. When I initially stopped my acting out behaviors and was not sexual for a time I felt the following: One night I laid on my bed, my legs ached like I had a severe cold or flue, my mind raced, and I pounded the bed to keep from masturbating. I needed my fix. I had

69

had these same physical feelings before but would preempt any further discomfort by using masturbation to stop the withdrawal symptoms. Now I had to go through them not knowing where they would lead. I managed to get through the night and attended a meeting the next day. Someone asked if I worked out in a gym and suggested that I get some physical exercise to cope with physical withdrawal. I began to go to the gym when there weren't many people there (women dressed in exercise clothing that I was attracted to). I got relief form the physical withdrawal and I began to take more suggestions from recovering people in my group.(see Bruce Browns *Understanding 12 Step Programs at http://understanding12stepprograms.com/*)

Some have varied symptoms of physical withdrawal from sex but the idea is to talk with those who have gone before you and who have faced these problems and gotten through them without acting out sexually or in other ways (with alcohol, drugs-prescriptions or illicit, gambling, over eating, spending, etc.).

Answer the following questions concerning withdrawal. Write out your answers. Explain each.

1) Do I feel out of sorts since I've limited or stopped my worst compulsive sexual behaviors?

_____

_____

_____

_____

2) Am I forgetting things or feeling confused somewhat about things in my life that I normally handled in the past?

_____

_____

_____

_____

3) Do I feel angry at times or do I feel peace? Does that seem out of character for me?

_____

_____

_____

_____

4) Do I experience agitation, hurt feelings or resentment (anger re-thought) easily.

_____

_____

_____

_____

5) Do I feel anxiety more than usual (anxious or fearful about the past, present or future)?

_____

_____

_____

_____

6) Do I feel depressed more than usual (crying easily, feeling lowly, low self-worth)?

_____

_____

_____

_____

7) Do I feel physically tired more than usual?

_____

_____

_____

_____

8) Do I have aches in my body that I didn't notice as much before?

_____

_____

_____

_____

9) Are my muscles more tense than usual (jaw, face, neck, back, stomach, etc)?

_____

_____

_____

_____

10) Are my thoughts jumbled or fuzzy at times?

_____

_____

_____

_____

11) Am I experiencing mood swings lately or do I feel suicidal?

_____

_____

_____

_____

_____

12) Have I had acting out dreams, fearful dreams, euphoric recall, or fantasies different than usual ? Do I have trouble sleeping?

_____

_____

_____

_____

○ While experiencing symptoms of withdrawal we make an effort to take care of ourselves. Remember that we are just beginning recovery from a life threatening disease and just like recovery from cancer or a heart attack, we need to treat withdrawal from sexual compulsion seriously. We practice the 15 second relaxation breathing technique as we need.

13) Am I getting plenty of rest or making time in my schedule to rest?

_____

_____

_____

_____

14) Do I need to seek advice from a professional (doctor, counselor etc.)?

_____

_____

_____

_____

15) Am I using the tools of the program to help calm me and get through withdrawal (telephone, meetings, slogans, reading recovery material, journaling etc.)?

_____

_____

_____

_____

16) Am I using the Serenity Prayer? (There is no requirement to believe anything but you may want to repeat this prayer written in the front of this book as an aid for calming thoughts and emotional stress. We can't think of two things at once)

_____

_____

_____

_____

17) Have I called my sponsor or another recovering sex addict today for support (sharing our withdrawal and difficulties or sharing our victories)?

_____

_____

_____

_____

18) Have I started to exercise on a regular basis? (This may require consulting a physician for some.)

_____

_____

_____

_____

19) Withdrawal may last for a few days or a few weeks or a few months. Am I aware that many sex addicts have experienced withdrawal and that it is possible to get through it without acting out?

_____

_____

_____

_____

More help concerning withdrawal is available in sexual support groups. You can find information on withdrawal in sexual addiction literature from those groups. (See Appendix III)

Managing Feelings

We can develop techniques for managing our new-found feelings and thinking and for practicing balance as we work through the 12 Steps. Many recovering sex addicts utilize the tools of our program to create more balance in their lives. These tools have been passed down by those who preceded us.

Sharing with our sponsor and in meetings with other recovering people is one of the most powerful tools to regaining our balance when we are emotionally upset. Sharing our difficulties or listening to someone share has a calming affect on the sufferer. None of us are immune to emotional upset. Old-timers as well as newcomers use this tool of *sharing* to calm our frayed nerves. If we can't meet face to face (f2f), we use the phone or perhaps E-mail or text someone to make contact.

The problem for some of us is: getting used to reaching out to others for help. If we practice calling recovering people on a regular basis, this daily practice will help to insure that we will make this necessary contact when we have problems. A member of the program shared: "I was told by a sponsor that I could break the ice when I called others by saying, '*Hi, I'm Bill and I'm just practicing calling.*' This may seem silly to some but it broke the ice for me, and has worked for many who had reservations about conversing with someone not familiar to them." This contact may even lead to new friendships.

Here are some tools for management of feelings:

1. Journaling / writing a stressor list
2. Our Higher Power / prayer and meditation
3. Using the two circles to define our addictive and ritual thoughts & behaviors (see Ch. 4)
4. Reading recovery literature
5. Now working the 12 Steps, meeting with a sponsor on a regular basis.
6. Apply Slogans to our life situations
7. Listening – Sharing at a meeting, by phone, or E-mail, etc
8. Pray the Serenity Prayer/meditation
9. Abstinence from addictive circle behaviors (Ch. 4) / use the *three second pause* (see Ch. 2)
10. Sponsoring, helping others, service work
11. Opening or Attending meetings with other recovering sex addicts
12. Needed Physical exercise / relaxation breathing

The actions above make up our program and we begin to establish a routine as we use these tools. This routine helps us to maintain sexual sobriety.

Answer the following questions (NOTE: Step 2 will address a Higher Power in a later chapter):

20) Do I agree or disagree that working the 12 Steps is a spiritual program? Why or why not?

_____

_____

_____

_____

21) In what ways am I abstaining from compulsive behavior?

_____

_____

_____

_____

_____

_____

22) Have I made recovery my priority and in what ways? Explain.

_____

_____

_____

_____

23) Am I open-minded in regards to recovery and suggestions of others? Describe.

_____

_____

_____

24) How am I willing to go to any length to get and stay sober? (use the twelve tools as a guide)

_____

_____

_____

_____

25) Have I noticed that I am more honest with myself or others? In what ways?

_____

_____

_____

26) It is wise to avoid people, places, and things involved in our acting out. Have I begun to seek safe places and safe people who enhance my recovery? Example: Avoiding TV or Internet hits, acting out partners or establishments etc. Describe.

_____

_____

_____

_____

27) Am I using the Serenity Prayer or the slogans in times of stress and in what ways?

_____

_____

_____

_____

28) Have I consistently tried some of the twelve tools listed above and did they help?

_____

_____

_____

_____

***Assignment*: For the next few days monitor your feelings and your self-talk and see what you can identify. If the feeling isn't on the list of *constructive or destructive* feelings above, add it to the list. Go over these feelings, you have noticed, with your sponsor or another recovering person. You may say "This is a lot of work." It may be, but ask yourself, "How much is your life worth?"**

We perform actions that change the way we think and feel. We go to any length to stay sane and sexually sober. We make calls and allow others to call us. We become willing to work through the steps. If we go to any length to get and stay sober from our compulsive sexual behaviors, our thinking begins to change. Remember that when the urge to act out comes, "This Too Shall Pass." It may take a few minutes, hours or a few days but it will pass.

This is our hope: "That our whole attitude and outlook upon life will begin to change. We will know a new freedom and a new happiness, we will intuitively know how to handle situations that used to baffle us, and we will not regret the past or wish to shut the door on it. (In working the 12 Step recovery process, there are other changes that will materialize if we work for them). Keep coming back" This is taken from the Promises, found in the book *Alcoholics Anonymous,* page 83 and 84, referring to Step 9.

One other caveat in recovery: We never compare our *insides* with someone's *outsides* – we make steady progress and avoid comparing ourselves to others.

If you are more interested in feelings and thought process in addiction and recovery, I recommend the book *Light in the Darkness* by St. George Lee. Call 757-595-0367 for more information.

_____

Program Check

So far you may have added several actions to your program of sobriety:

Q. Are you going to at least one meeting a week or receiving help with your addiction to sex? (Yes)   (No)

Q. Do you know who your sponsor is? (Yes)   (No)

Q. Do you have a few phone numbers of members of sexual recovery groups and are you making phone calls? (Yes)   (No)

Q. Are you reading sexual recovery material? (Yes)   (No)

Q. Do you have a daily meditation book for sex addiction and are you using it? (Yes)   (No)

Q. Are you listing your stressors (as bullets) weekly (the beginning of journaling)? (Yes)   (No)

Q. Are you making a daily sobriety plan (mental notes or written)?

Q. Are you using the 12 Tools to manage feelings?

Do you have any holes in your program so far – are you missing any of these tools? Our program is only as good as our actions. If you need to, stop here and take care of these holes before moving on. This is the "*work*" part of the workbook. Sometimes, people travel great distances to go to meetings and find it worthwhile. If you are situated such that you cannot make a meeting, call or go online and contact a sexual recovery group for help. Sooner or later you may be able to start a meeting in your area.

At this time please take a 45 second Serenity Break:

_____

45 second serenity break

Rest for a few moments…… relax…

Take a deep breath, hold a few seconds and let it out and relax......

Allow your body to relax; ...your legs, ...your stomach, ...your jaw, chest and back, ...shoulders, ... arms, ...neck, ...face.

Now let your mind relax. Calm – be still and just be.

Repeat this several times and then stop your exercise. Now see how that feels as you participated in this exercise

Use this technique during a stressful time.

In the next chapter we will define our sobriety while working Step 1.

Process of Sexual Recovery

.

PART 2: THE STABILIZATION STEPS
Steps 1, 2 & 3

Process of Sexual Recovery

STEP 1

_____

Process of Sexual Recovery

CHAPTER 4

STEP 1

Defining Our Addiction

The Solution: The 12 Steps is our answer to the problem of sexual addiction. It exposes us to recovery and a Higher Power. When we work through the steps we are not looking for our self-esteem. Self-esteem is a *byproduct* of working the 12 Step program. We are seeking sexual sobriety.

Step one may be written as: *Admitted that we were powerless over our addictive and/or compulsive sexual behavior (or addiction) – that our lives had become unmanageable.* This step was rewritten by some groups recovering from sex addiction but was originally developed by AA in the 1930's for recovery from alcoholism. Alcoholics Anonymous is the father of all 12 Step programs. The power of these steps has survived during those years through war and crisis and has been passed down to other 12 Step groups including groups for recovery from sexual addiction. Most of these programs and their recovery processes have been derived from AA as is this workbook.

When we *define our addiction,* we begin to understand areas of our lives that are out of control. We are powerless to stop or change them without help from others who understand. We discover, through the process of defining our addiction, by using the two circles, just how unmanageable our lives have become. When a life is constantly in chaos and upheaval, either emotionally or physically, life is out of control and it is usually difficult to manage important aspects of it. We are powerless to stop our compulsive sexual behavior and we need help.

Look at help from other sex addicts in this way: If we go to a medical doctor and ask to have a tooth pulled, then we are asking someone who may not understand. On the other hand, if we go to a dentist to fix our broken leg the same applies. Either way, we have gone to someone who may not be able to help. So it is appropriate that we ask for help in defining our problem with sex addiction from someone who has been there and knows about a solution that worked for them and many others. We may have different sexual problems but we have a common solution – We seek help from other recovering sex addicts and incorporate the 12 Steps and our Higher Power into our recovery.

(We acknowledge and thank Patrick Carnes for his work developing the levels of sexual addiction found in the book *Out of The Shadows.* These levels show the progression of sexual disease and help us define our addiction.) In this work book we use this example to develop our circles.

The Circle of Life

Step 1 for recovery from any addiction may best be worked by using our circles below as a guide to defining our sobriety. These two circles were mentioned in previous chapters concerning our sexual addiction. There is nothing mysterious about them. They're not crop circles. Rather, they are two circles that may be used as a tool in our recovery from this disease. They give us a bird's eye view to help monitor our addiction.

Imagine flying over a field and we look down and see a bull's eye and something written in it. The *addictive circle*, the center circle says "Danger, don't go there-this is where we act out," We call the next circle outward the *ritual circle.* It says "Caution, this may lead directly back to the addictive circle." On the outside of the circles we call this our *growth area.* It says "Green light, you're in a free zone, this is where life begins and you're in the right place!!" The growth area is *The Circle Of Life*: **This** **is where we want to get to - where we want to live.**

We use common sense in making our list of what goes into each circle saving our worst behaviors for the addictive circle and other less destructive ones for our ritual circle. The growth area should contain those things that are non-addictive in nature and that enhance our lives. The growth area keeps us out of our unhealthy behaviors.

How do the circles help us with Step 1? Step one is about being powerless over our addiction and compulsiveness toward sexual thoughts and behaviors. These two circles hold the truth about our powerlessness. Our lives become out of control, unmanageable when we act on these behaviors. In the example below the person with these behaviors has voyeur problems and engages in anonymous sex as well. These addictive circle behaviors are those behaviors that cause chaos and trouble (unmanageability) in our lives to the extent that we need to abstain from them. The ritual circle items can arouse the *addict within* and lead us toward behaviors in our addictive circle.

Below shows a picture of what our circles may look like. You can easily see, by examining closely, why the growth area is important. The list of behaviors and activities can vary greatly. It is basically up to the person to decide what goes into each. It may be wise to run it by your sponsor or a person in recovery who has used this tool and is comfortable sharing with you. In the beginning we keep it simple and only put the behaviors that effect us most and later we add more. Here is an example of what could go in each:

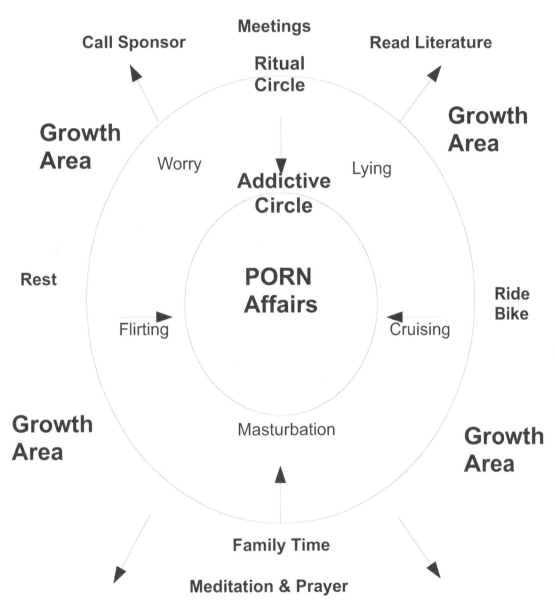

We define our two circles with the help of a sponsor or someone in recovery from sexual addiction. If we complete this process alone, we may skip items that should go on our list. Our tendency to isolate may make us want to do it alone. It is best, however, to receive help from people who understand sexual compulsiveness. *Study the example above closely* to get an idea of what might go in each circle for you. This is an example only. While this example gives you a general idea of what types of behaviors go in each circle, you will likely have different items to add or subtract.

In entering items into our growth area, we sometimes have difficulty thinking of what to write. Most of us have let go of our hobbies and interests and replaced them with sexual activities or have used them in an effort to be sexual. Sex became the center of our life, the alpha and omega, and became our entire focus. Be sure to place, in the growth area, items like *recovery meetings, reading recovery literature, sponsorship, recovery tools*; items that enhance our recovery. We also may enter into our growth area hobbies we want to try or things like going on healthy dates with our spouse or significant other, getting out in nature, getting a puppy or other pet, play time with children. We add new behaviors like: developing a sense of humor. If not in a period of celibacy, we even add healthy sex.

As you can see from the example above, the Ritual Circle leads back towards the Addictive Circle (our core addictive behaviors) while the Growth Area leads away from compulsive behavior (this Growth Area is also referred to as "Beyond the Circles.") So the more we engage in positive actions the further away from sexual acting out we get. This disease affects us mentally, physically, spiritually, and emotionally so we keep in mind that the Growth Area needs to have these elements in it. We get physical exercise of some sort and connect with nature (again-you may need to consult your physician). We participate in family time and recovery meetings, we develop our talents, and we connect with our spiritual needs as well. The Growth Area extends indefinitely away from our sexual problems as long as we stay with the program. It has no bounds and is not confined as long as it is within the framework of the 12 Steps.

After carefully looking over this example, draw two circles or use the ones provided below and make your first attempt at entering items into each. You don't have to be perfect when choosing the items for your list. You can add, subtract, or move items later. In time and with the help of your sponsor and your new recovering friends, you can develop this into a useful tool and get a bird's eye view of your disease and of the solution: living by the 12 Steps and living in *The Circle of Life...* beyond the circles.

1) From the previous work done in question 2 of Chapter 1 use the *a to z list* of categories of compulsive sexual behaviors to generate your own *addictive circle* behaviors. Draw the circles and make your entries (most are hand drawn and hand written or you may use the example provided below - they don't have to look perfect).

2) Use the *a to z list* of categories of obsessive thoughts and behaviors in question 10 of chapter 1 (leading to acting out) to generate your own *ritual circle* behaviors. Place these in the circle provided.

3) If we choose we can use these circles to guide us towards more healthy sexual interaction and balance. We use our growth area to move forward in our recovery. List healthy items and behaviors that you are doing now, that you would like to do in the future, or that you have done in the past as possible growth area behaviors that can empower you. Place these on the outside of the two circles. (Use the a to z list below to help you with hobby and interest entries for your growth area). Be sure to place 12 Step program recovery items in it. If all else fails, as Humphrey Bogart might have said, *keep it simple sweetheart* (K.I.S.S).

We can have power brought into our daily sober walk with these growth area items. Consider them carefully and when it feels right in your gut write them down. The growth behaviors don't have to be acted upon all at once. We gradually introduce them into our life's schedule. On the next page we find our two circles.

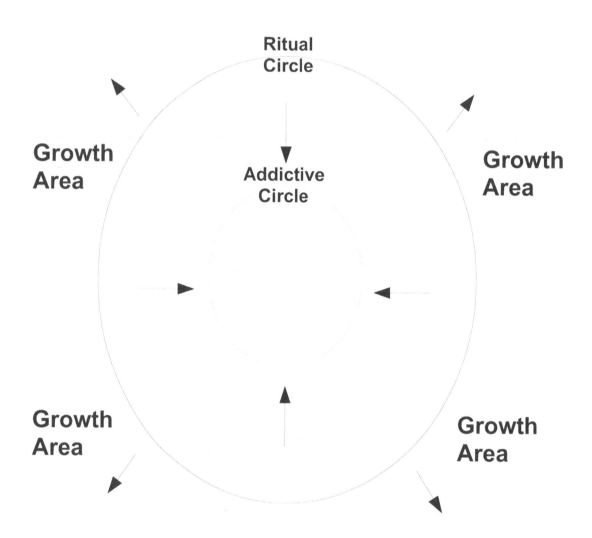

Growth Area List

Here is an *a to z hobby list* to aid you in making additional entries into your growth area:

a. Arts and crafts (song, dance, art, sculpture, ceramics, origami, comedian etc.)
b. Cars, boats, airplanes (antiques, rebuild, learn to operate etc.)
c. Church, religious or spiritual involvement (Remember balance!)
d. Taking or teaching a class
e. Collecting or trading
f. Computer (e.g., set up a family web site or join an Internet support group, computer art and more)
g. Cooking
h. DIY (do it your self) building, refurbishing (furniture, etc.)
i. Electronics
j. Film-making (non-addictive)
k. Games (cards, chess, scrabble etc.) Groups or clubs (online, in person)
l. Gardening (flower, vegetable etc.)
m. Literature (reading or writing a book, articles, publishing)
n. Mentor or helping others, visiting the elderly, meals on wheels, coaching soccer (unless children have been an addictive part of your past) etc.
o. Models (cars, planes, doll houses, etc.)
p. Music (non-addictive)
q. Outdoor activities (tennis, walks in the forest, hiking, jogging, swimming, fishing etc.)
r. Pet (raise, breed, show etc.)
s. Photography (non-sexual)
t. Puzzles
u. Researching (genealogy, history, etc.)
v. Sports / physical activities, exercise
w. Touring, sightseeing
x. Toys (build, collect, etc.)
y. Volunteer work (Be sure not to over extend yourself in this or any other area.)
z. Watch collector, coins, pens etc.

Answer the following questions and explain each.

4) Are there items or issues that I am holding back and have not disclosed to others or not added to my addictive or ritual circle because I am ashamed of them? List them.

_____

_____

_____

_____

5) Have I only listed convenient items in my circles and held back some that I don't want to stop that should be listed? List them here and add them to your circles.

_____

_____

_____

_____

6) It takes time to develop the growth area. Are there hobbies or interests that were discarded in the past that are potentially items that could go into the growth area. We list even ones we don't think we can do anymore because of physical ability or time deprivation (there may be other forms of these hobbies or interests available to us).

_____

_____

_____

_____

○ Come back to this section and add more growth area items that you develop or draw circles in a separate place and keep it handy to enter these new-found patterns. Some use a poster board for their two circles, keep it where they can see it, and use it as a reminder of what changes they want to make. Whatever you decide to do, keep it simple and don't complicate the process. If complicated, it may lead to discouragement or failure. Easy does it. . . but do it.

7) Have I consulted another recovering sex addict (s) in addition to my sponsor for ideas and guidance? Why or why not? What was their feedback?

_____

_____

_____

_____

8) Are there past or ongoing illegal activities that may prohibit me from completing my circles? It may be wise to *code* these behaviors so that you are the only one who knows their meaning in order to keep them private. You might only share them with your sponsor, counselor and those you trust with this information. (NOTE: We are not advocating hiding illegal activities so much as keeping sensitive information from those who may not understand the nature of recovery. If there is past or ongoing illegal activity you may also need professional help.)

_____

_____

_____

_____

o Sometimes issues from the past surface. Randy, a member of a sexual recovery group, spoke with his mother and was told about a sexual abuse issue from his childhood that he had forgotten or blocked from memory for decades. This added perspective helped him in his path of recovery.

9) Have I spoken to family and friends about my condition, and if so are there issues from my past that I wasn't aware of or that seem fuzzy in my memory?

_____

_____

_____

_____

10) What is my best non-sexual positive memory from childhood?

_____

_____

_____

_____

11) Are there talents from my childhood, like singing, art, service to others, etc., that I haven't yet fully developed, which I may place as positive goals, interests or creativity in my growth area?

_____

_____

_____

_____

12) Are there classes I might enroll in (non-career fun classes) that I have creative interest in? (Sometimes these hobbies turn into careers for us).

_____

_____

_____

_____

13) Do you have a private interest which you haven't shared with anyone because of fear, low self-esteem or time deprivation, which may seem practically impossible to engage in, but for which you have a deep yearning? Example: writing a book, screen play or acting.

_____

_____

_____

_____

We may be over committed in some areas of our lives and we may have to reduce our involvement so we can make room for other activities that we want to try. Nothing is written in stone. We use good generalship (management and judgment) of our resources and time. We avoid a *get rich quick* attitude and turn our thoughts toward healthy activity and we *learn to play*. Many of us have worked hard all of our lives and have used sexual pursuit as our playgrounds. Now we exchange those familiar acting out behaviors for more wholesome endeavors.

The growth list above is for reference. There are probably more categories that can be added so use your imagination and have fun. Consider things that tweak your interests. Be bold in placing items on your list. If one of these don't work out then try another. Be careful of high risk activities; these may only be replacements for our risky acting out behavior. Remember that balance is important; we don't overdo work or play. It may sound boring because everything initially may seem to pale when compared to sexual activity, but there is *life after addiction*, abundant life through recovery using the 12 Steps.

Looking Back

We have dealt with our sexual disease (dis-ease – not at ease) as it applies to our lives today, but what about our past and its influence on our daily lives and our relations with people. Our past may have caused us problems that materialize in our present. We look into our past with the knowledge that it could be painful to experience the feelings that may accompany our search. This may require us to pursue counseling, professional help or treatment. Many recovering people use these services if we are situated to do so. You may want to discuss this with your sponsor or others in recovery that may have had similar experiences. Most may find this process can be achieved by sponsorship and going to meetings but if we are suicidal or have other problems that are best handles by professionals, then we seek their help.

Fear can be thought of as an acronym: F.E.A.R., *future events appearing real. W*e react to these fears as if they are actually happening at the moment we are thinking about them. We project into the future, events and situations, that may never even happen. We sometimes refer to this as "future tripping" or scriptwriting. We often use the past to project future outcomes. The steps have the effect of keeping us planted firmly in the present. In 12 Step programs there are a list of *promises* that take place during the ninth step. From this list of promises there is one that stands out. It states that *we will not regret the past nor wish to shut the door on it.* First we need to examine our past in order to avoid its controlling of our present. Below are a few questions to jog your memory. Slow down (easy does it), take your time and answer these questions thoughtfully and honestly.

14) What is my earliest memory as a child?

_____

_____

_____

_____

15) Is it a <u>negative</u> or <u>positive</u> memory for you? Circle one.

16) What kind of feelings does this memory generate?

_____

_____

_____

_____

17) At this point it is necessary to be aware that some of us gravitate only toward positive memories of our past and bury the negative. Conversely we may only focus on the negative, crowding out our positive experiences. If there was a negative memory that came to mind in question 1 or 14/15, think of a positive one as well. If the initial memory was positive, note the negative ones. We are seeking balance with this exercise.

_____

_____

_____

_____

18) Family History: Our experiences may vary widely from one another. One thing we have in common in our pasts is that we all had authority figures who guided us as we grew up (mother, father, relative, teacher and so on). Do you have good or bad feelings when you think of these authority figures and why? What happened? Did they have any addiction problems or do they presently?

Father

_____

_____

_____

_____

Mother

_____

_____

_____

_____

Sister (s)

_____

_____

_____

_____

_____

Brother (s)

_____

_____

_____

_____

_____

Grandmother

_____

_____

_____

_____

Grandfather

_____

_____

_____

_____

Uncle (s)

_____

_____

_____

_____

Aunt (s)

_____

_____

_____

_____

Other Relatives

_____

_____

_____

_____

_____

Family Friend (s)

_____

_____

_____

_____

_____

Teacher

_____

_____

_____

_____

_____

Clergy

_____

_____

_____

_____

_____

Stranger

_____

_____

_____

_____

Others

_____

_____

_____

_____

19) Who stands out in the above exercise (question 18)? Expand on your encounters with him, her or them of both a positive and negative nature.

Negative_____

_____

_____

_____

_____

_____

Positive_____

_____

_____

_____

_____

_____

○ These individuals helped shape our present thinking and behaviors either positively or negatively. At this point it is wise to remember that we don't blame others for our addictive behavior and our lot in life. While we do acknowledge how we were influenced by these people, we realize that we are responsible for our own recovery. We *face everything and recover*.

20) Do I have resentments (anger re-thought or grudges) towards these people who affected me in a less than positive way? Explain.

_____

_____

_____

_____

21) Am I ashamed to have a normal conversation about how I grew up or about my past? Explain.

_____

_____

_____

_____

○ There was a speaker who helped distribute spiritual literature behind the iron curtain (former USSR controlled territory) who said "What would you do or allow your children to do if you didn't have fear." Some fear is healthy when it comes to survival but we, as sex addicts, have taken this fearful thought process into every aspect of our lives. One member shared, "My mother told us to be afraid of anything or anyone new to us, and I passed this on to my children."

22) Are there any irrational fears learned from past from authority figures or in childhood that I now practice or am passing on to my children or to others?

_____

_____

_____

_____

23) Are these fears holding me back from doing new things like participating in life fully or developing new interests or hobbies that enhance my life?

_____

_____

_____

_____

24) Was there jealousy or envy on my part from the past that are active in my life today? With whom? What was the reason (s)?

_____

_____

_____

_____

o Many of us reacted to our childhood trauma or perceived trauma in a way that caused us to compensate. We compensated by overeating, spending, fighting, blaming, resenting, acting out with drugs, alcohol, sex, and other compulsive behaviors, and more.

25) Do I have any other behaviors or thinking besides sexual dysfunction that influenced my past or that may be influencing my present?

_____

_____

_____

_____

o Some people who do not have a problem with alcohol begin to moderate drinking to keep from lowering their sexual inhibitions too much and start their addiction going again. Drugs may also have the same affect on sex addicts as well as other addictive nonsexual behaviors.

26) Make a chronology (list by age) of milestones you remember as you grew up. Here is an example:

Age 5   Father and mother separated
Age 6   Started school
Age 10   Moved to another state with grandparents
Age 12   Had female cousin masturbated me
Age 14   Won baseball trophy
Age 15   Began drinking, smoking
Age 17   Had first sexual intercourse with female professor
Age 18   Got married - wife 10 years older than me
Age 21   Finished college and entered military service
Age 28   Became a commercial pilot
Age 32   Wife found out about my acting out on the job
Age 35   Was caught again and wife informed my boss
Age 35   Attended my first 12 Step meeting for sexual addiction
Age 36   Began working the steps with a sponsor.

Now make a list, to the best of your recollection, of milestones in your life.

_____

_____

_____

_____

_____

_____

_____

_____

_____

_____

_____

_____

_____

_____

_____

_____

○ This list of milestones above can be expanded and used as an outline for writing our first step and presenting it to our sponsor or in some cases our sexual recovery group. (You may find it helpful to ask parents, siblings, and friends you grew up with for input.) Refer to this outline when you write out your 1ˢᵗ Step below.

Writing and Presenting The 1ˢᵗ Step

When writing our 1ˢᵗ Step, we review the past work we have done in this workbook for reference. We use our list of milestones to write out our story, including our sexual behaviors, in chronological order from our earliest memories to the present. Our goal is to show the *progression* of our sexual compulsive or addictive behavior along with other inappropriate behaviors. We tell *how it was* in the past, *what happened* when we hit bottom and *what it's like now* in recovery (tell what things you do to stay sober today – work the steps, meditate, pray, journal); basically go over your growth area recovery behaviors as well as your life events). At the beginning of your story describe your family of origin and any compulsive behaviors that were/are present in your father, mother, grandparents, siblings, aunts, uncles, cousins, etc. If you have knowledge of it, describe the state of your family when you were born. (Ask family members for information). The stories we present to our group or our sponsor will be detailed but we don't want to get caught up in the details.

After completing the first draft of our story, we ask our sponsor or other recovering sex addicts, who have worked a first step, to give us feedback on our work. Allow suggestions from others. The point of this review is to insure that we use appropriate, non-triggering language but also that we tell the truth about our lives. We tell on the addict. It may be helpful to listen to

108

someone's 1st Step to get an idea of how you want to present yours. Speaking to one who has recently presented a 1st step may also be helpful.

The principle of Step 1 is: SURRENDER

When you and your sponsor are confident you are finished writing your presentation, you may, in some sexual recovery groups, make an appointment with your home group to present your 1st Step to the group at a meeting. As you share your first step with the group or your sponsor, allow the feelings to surface. If you feel like crying, it's OK. Laughter may also take place during your presentation. Many of us have experienced feelings we have suppressed for too long when we do such things as presenting our 1st Step. You are not merely reporting to the group. In this exercise feel the feelings as they surface without stuffing them back down. We share our feelings with our friends in recovery as well as events.

Write you sobriety date here (the day you completed Step 1):_____.

_____

Program Check

So far you may have added several more actions to your program of sobriety:

You are going to at least one meeting a week or receiving help with your addiction to sex and are working Step 1 (abstinent from addictive sexual behaviors).   (Yes)   (No)

You know who your sponsor is. (Yes)   (No)

You have a few phone numbers of members of you sexual recovery group and are making phone calls. (Yes)   (No)

You are reading sexual addiction recovery literature and the meditation book *Answers in the Heart*. (Yes)   (No)

Q. Are you journaling or writing a weekly stressor list? (Yes)   (No)

Q. Are you making mental notes of your feelings? (Yes)   (No)

Q. Are you making daily sobriety plans to get through the day without acting out?

(Yes)   (No)

Q. Are you aware that you may still be going through physical or emotional withdrawal?
(Yes)   (No)

Take a *Serenity Break* for approximately one minute before moving on. You deserve it! You have completed much work and you have grown in your recovery.

Take a 1 minute serenity break

Rest for a few moments......relax...you may choose to close your eyes.

Take a deep breath, hold and let it out completely at once and relax......

Allow your body to relax; ...your legs, ...your stomach, ...your jaw, chest and back, ...shoulders, ... arms, ...neck, ...face..your eyes.

Now let your mind relax. Calm – be still and just be.

Repeat this several times then stop your exercise.

Use this technique during a stressful time and monitor your body as you practice this. You may be sitting or standing and some take long walks and practice relaxing.

Now that you have listed your behaviors in the your circles, have discussed your past and have written and presented your 1st Step, let us now turn our attention to Step 2.

KJ Nivin

STEP 2

CHAPTER 5

STEP 2

Defining Our Higher Power

Step 2 states: *Came to believe that a power greater than ourselves could restore us to sanity.* There is much to think about in this step. First let us examine the spirit of the 2ⁿᵈ Step.

In Step 2, we don't concern ourselves with such matters as: Which came first, the chicken or the egg? Our job in this step is to get off the debating team and examine for ourselves what is real to us.

In the beginning we *came* (came to meetings), *came to* (came to our senses) and *came to believe* (believe in a power greater than ourselves). Then it was necessary for us to admit that our behavior and thinking were leading to insanity. Finally we came to believe that a power greater than ourselves (a Higher Power) could bring us back to a sane state of mind. We can't start out flatfooted and expect to jump this hurdle of belief in a Higher Power or to admit insanity all in one hour. This may take time for us. This is a process. The most important thing is to 'stop analyzing and start utilizing.'

To utilize Step 2 it is best to start out with an *open mind*, the key necessary aspect to working this step. We examine each part of the step. There are plenty of issues that will influence our ability to believe in a power greater than ourselves. Some of us grew up in religious families, some had no religious backgrounds whatsoever and some are somewhere in between. Our backgrounds play a big part in our forming an idea of a Higher Power.

As stated in a previous chapter, some who have trouble with the concept of a power greater than ourselves begin with the recovery group as a Higher Power. It is our experience that God does work through people. The group is made up of sex addicts working together to stay sexually sober. The group working together is certainly a power greater than each of us alone. In Step 2, we come to realize that there is a power great than ourselves who can help us, whatever the initial form of that power. As recovery (and spirituality) progresses, our *idea* of the nature of our Higher Power is likely to change.

Some have believed in a Higher Power their entire lives and they wonder why they couldn't stay away from acting out even though they had established their belief years before. Some had at best a nebulous knowledge of a Higher Power, but they know that addiction was killing them. Whatever the case, we need to consider a concept of a Higher Power. We need a *faith* that works.

We will begin by answering some questions to get the thinking process started. As before, write your answers out. You get out of this work what you put into it.

1) Do I have preconceived ideas about a Higher Power (either pro or con)? Example: Church upbringing, authority figures' influence etc. What are some of your old ideas about a Higher Power?

_____

_____

_____

_____

○ The old ideas we are referring to don't have anything to do with finding or switching religions. This discussion is geared toward ideas we have developed about our *concept* of God in the past which don't still work for us today. Obviously, whether we are religious or not, these ideas we developed over the years haven't helped when it came to staying sexually sober. We need to be open to new ways of using our Higher Power's help to become and remain sober.

2) Do these ideas about a Higher Power cause me to want to isolate from the group or from reaching out? Explain.

_____

_____

_____

_____

3) How do I feel when I hear people talking about their Higher Power or about God? Am I indifferent? Do I find myself negative or judgmental or do I find myself comfortable during discussions about a Higher Power or a little bit of each?

_____

_____

_____

_____

4) Am I baffled, even though I have developed a concept of God as I understand God, that I can't stay sexually sober?

_____

_____

_____

_____

5) As stated before, we need a faith that works. Am I willing to let go of old ideas about a Higher Power or modify them into something that works for me? Explain.

_____

_____

_____

_____

6) In the past, as a child, were there situations or events that occurred that helped shape my ideas of God as I understand God (or don't understand God). Explain.

_____

_____

_____

_____

7) Am I judgmental toward those who have developed a faith or whose faith is different from mine?

_____

_____

_____

_____

8) Do I agree that, in having a concept of a Higher Power, it would have to be a concept that would help me stay sober? Explain.

_____

_____

_____

_____

9) Am I willing to discuss my concept with another recovering sex addict or with my sponsor in order to gain more of an understanding of a Higher Power?

_____

_____

_____

_____

10) We aren't required to believe in anything, but it is suggested that we keep an open mind. If I don't have a power greater than myself that helps me to stay sexually sober, am I willing to accept help and guidance from others? Explain.

_____

_____

_____

_____

11) If I had a choice of how I would like a Higher Power to be towards me, would I choose a loving, helpful Higher Power, one that is non-judgmental and affirming? What would my (new?) concept be?

_____

_____

_____

_____

The reason we need to re-evaluate our position concerning God as we understand Him is so that we can develop a working relationship with God. For many of us this working relationship has become important in helping keep us sexually sober. It is suggested that we begin *to act as if*. We act as if we believe, by trying out new ways to think about this power greater than ourselves, and we begin to take action, *as if* we believed. One recovering person looks at God as love and tries to show that love toward people. By developing these new ideas, we may act our way into a new way of thinking.

The actions we take can be many and varied, as long as we take action ("Merely saying I'M TRYING doesn't always work!"). We stop our debating and start seeking answers. One person was instructed to place her shoes under her bed at night. When she knelt to do so, she was reminded to say *thank you*. In the morning when she knelt down to retrieve her shoes, she was told to say *please help me*. She didn't have to believe anything. She merely had to follow instructions. In doing so, she was demonstrating a form of faith. All she had to do was to wait and observe the changes this new behavior brought about.

She reported later that things in her life began to change without her actually trying to create the changes. She used this flimsy reed of an idea as the center of her life in early recovery. She is now sober for some time. She states that this technique helped her to stop analyzing and to start utilizing the tools presented to her.

12) If I have had little or no concept of God in the past, am I now willing to try this simple form of prayer? Explain how you would implement this into your daily life.

_____

_____

_____

_____

13) If I have had a concept of a Higher Power in the past, but was unable to stay sober, am I willing to try the example above by simply saying *thank you* at night and *help me* in the morning? Explain what might hold you back.

_____

_____

_____

_____

14) Change is difficult for many of us. Am I now willing to stop doing things my way and to try out new ideas?

_____

_____

_____

_____

15) If I am not willing to make changes in my old ideas of a Higher Power, how do I expect to stay sexually free of compulsion?

_____

_____

_____

_____

16) We look to those who have preceded us and who have a program of recovery that works. Our way hasn't worked for us in the past. Am I willing to admit that recovering sex addicts have a way to stay sober that may work for me as well? Explain.

_____

_____

_____

_____

There are several parts to this step as mentioned above. We have discussed the possibility of a Higher Power working in our lives. Some will want to shy away from this subject. We are not offering religious instruction or changing religions, we advocate changing our relationship to that Power. If you don't have a concept of a Higher Power, we are talking about choosing a Higher Power as we understand this Power, a Power who will work on our behalf. Remember that the keys to this program are *honesty, open-mindedness and willingness (H.O.W.)*. This 2nd Step requires us to be open-minded. We look to others to find a faith that works for us and this takes humility on our part (the state or quality of being humble; absence of pride or self-assertion).

Next we will focus on the idea that we had become insane when it came to sex. Insanity is defined here as *doing the same things over and over and getting the same result while expecting the results to be different each time.* Sexual acting out is the insane thing we keep doing over and over, and we keep getting the same results: an unmanageable out-of-control life. We act out on our addictive behaviors and when we don't get the results we want we try the same behaviors all over again or the same patterns of our addiction. We act out sexually and the vicious cycle continues. Isn't this insanity at its worst?

Our insanity grows as the disease of sexual addiction progresses.

17) In looking back on my past, how have I been insane as far as my addiction is concerned. What are some insane behaviors I have done?

_____

_____

_____

_____

18) Have I become frustrated or resentful that my life isn't / wasn't going well under its present management?

_____

_____

_____

_____

19) Who have I hurt with my anger or how have I caused confusion by my patterns of acting out sexually or have I been a phony presenting a good face but knowing I didn't deserve it.

_____

_____

_____

_____

20) Have I had lapses in my thinking – forgotten things or misjudged situations? Has this gotten worse compared to the past? (Is my insanity progressing?)

_____

_____

_____

_____

21) Did I become angry or mean-spirited when denied sex or the type of sex I wanted?

_____

_____

_____

_____

22) How do I treat store clerks or other people I meet in my every day life? Do I talk down to them or treat them in a less than loving way? Do I try to attract them for sex? (If unaware of these behaviors, monitor your future behavior when encountering these people)?

_____

_____

_____

_____

23) Do I agree that I may have gone too far in making my wishes known concerning sex (the type, the frequency etc.)?

_____

_____

_____

_____

24) Am I willing to concede that I have been insane when it came to my sex conduct?

_____

_____

_____

_____

       We may admit that we have acted insane in our sex lives, but what about the rest of our lives. Didn't we have to tell lies to cover up the lies to cover up the lie we told to begin with? Haven't we lived a *double life* and been dishonest in many ways? We didn't ever want our actions to see the light of day. We wanted others to perceive us in a certain way knowing that we didn't deserve it. We wanted the reputation of being *the good guy* but knew we were phonies.

25) In what ways have I been dishonest or insane in my dealings with others (close or casual relationships)?

_____

_____

_____

_____

26) Have I lied and covered up my compulsive sexual behaviors? Explain.

_____

_____

_____

_____

27) Do I now think that deceit was part of my addiction and insane behavior?

_____

_____

_____

_____

28) Have I stolen time from work to act out (even in small ways – i.e. leaving work to get sex, being late for work, working at half steam, or acting out at work on the computer, flirting or masturbating etc.)

_____

_____

_____

_____

29) Many of us risked our jobs, careers and livelihood to act out. We stood a chance of getting fired or losing our reputations. Have I lost or risked losing these things?

_____

_____

_____

_____

30) Have I risked losing family and friends to pursue my addiction? Have I experienced these kinds of losses in my distant or recent past?

_____

_____

31) Do I consider these unnecessary risks to be a part of my insanity?

_____

_____

_____

_____

_____

_____

We can see if we have answered these questions honestly, that there is insanity in our lives concerning sex as well as in other areas. We now begin to understand our life was influenced by insane behavior and thinking. We begin to accept that a life run on insane thinking is a life doomed to failure. We come to the part now about believing that a power greater than ourselves can and will restore us to sanity.

Above we talked about believing in or developing a belief in God as we understand God. Now we take it a step further. We need to consider believing that God can and will help us get and stay sexually sober as we cooperate in our recovery. Cooperation is our part in our relationship with a Higher Power.

Look around your recovery support meetings. Are there people staying sane and sober from sexual compulsion? Most aren't perfect but they indicate that they are better off than they were before they got into recovery. Most have developed a concept of a Higher Power that works for them. We now have to admit that God or their idea of God is doing for them what they couldn't do for themselves. We now begin to accept the idea that if it is working for them, it could probably work for us.

Can I choose my own concept of a Higher Power? Yes. In recovery we don't browbeat others into the only way they can consider a Higher Power. We look at our relationship with our Higher Power as a *personal* relationship. We choose a concept for a Higher Power that is comfortable for us, one that is loving and that we believe will work in our new way of life.. Some choose a Higher Power that has all of the attributes that we would like to have for ourselves. This power may be loving, kind, thoughtful, considerate, non-judgmental, honest, responsible, gentle and possess many other good traits. If our *concept* of our Higher power is that of a a judgmental god, we may trade our concept in for one who has the attributes mentioned. You choose.

In looking inward we may find that we are not as bad as we think, that perhaps we have been too hard on ourselves. There are others whose addiction has been more disabling than ours who have developed a good program of recovery. We use their example and latch on to the possibility that we may be restored to sanity. Many of us do recover if we have (or develop) the capacity to be honest – honest with ourselves and others in recovery. Honest about our disease.

We make deposits in our spiritual bank by going to meetings, working the steps, calling others in recovery, journaling, and adding more actions to our program of recovery. Then when the time comes to make a withdrawal to keep from acting out, we have the spiritual funds available to us to stay sober. We reach into our "Spiritual Bank"….to make withdrawals when we need to. Spirituality brings hope.

The principle of Step 2 is: HOPE.

This concludes our discussion on the 2nd Step but it will be necessary for you, as a recovering person, to pursue and develop your own concept of a power greater than yourself. You will need an idea of a Higher Power in order to move on to Step 3.

Before moving on, take a Serenity Break using the technique previously used. Have fun with it and really try to relax.

———————————————————

Program Check

So far you may have added even more actions to your program of sobriety:

You are going to at least one meeting a week and receiving help with your addiction to sex.

You have a sponsor.

You have a few phone numbers of members in recovery and are making phone calls.

You are reading sexual addiction recovery literature and a meditation book

You are journaling or writing a weekly stressor list and making daily sobriety plans to get through the day without acting out.

You are making mental note of your feelings.

You are practicing the "three second pause."

You are aware that you may still be going through physical or emotional withdrawal.

Q. Are you using the two circles to practice sexual sobriety?　(Yes)　(No)

Q. Do you have a belief in God as you understand God?　(Yes)　(No)

STEP 3

_____

KJ Nivin

CHAPTER 6

STEP 3

Turning It Over

By this point in our program we should be on the road to believing in a Power greater than ourselves, having addressed this in Step 2. We go from a *faith* that there *may* be spiritual help to: *knowing* that there is.

The 3rd Step builds off the 2nd Step. In this step, we decide to turn things in our life over to this Higher Power and eventually to turn our entire life over to the care of this power by working the rest of the 12 Steps.

Step 3 states: *Made a decision to turn our will and our life over to the care of God as we understood Him.* This step can be broken down into separate parts: First we'll consider the phrase *'made a decision.'* Then *'turn our will and life over'* : How *do* we turn our life over? Finally we need to decide what the phrase *'to the care of God'* means to us.

Defining Step Three

When we *make a decision* we may look at it as deciding to perform an action: If there are three frogs sitting on a log and one decides to jump off, how many are left? There are still three frogs left on the log. The one frog only *decided* to jump off, but it hasn't necessarily jumped yet. In this step, however, when we use the word 'decided or decision,' we also assume that there is action behind our decision. Otherwise, it won't have any affect on our lives. So, in the 3rd Step we make three decisions and then act on those decisions. We decide to be willing to allow our Higher Power (God as we understand God) to care for us. We also make a decision to stay calm and not to react to negative situations in our life. Finally, we make a decision to work the rest of the 12 Steps. After making these three decisions we go into action and do what is necessary to accomplish these tasks.

What about the words *will and life?* What do they mean to us? These words may seem vague or include too much. One member said that he initially had a problem finding more specific meaning out of these two words *will and life.* His sponsor came to the rescue by saying "Instead of saying we turned our will and life over to the care of God you might consider saying we turned our *thoughts and our decisions* over. Our thoughts include our will and our decisions make up our lives". This made sense to him and in terms he could understand.

The following is an example of *turning it over*: John is a sex addict and works in sales. John was told that there are going to be cuts in the work force and that he may be one of the people cut. John is recovering from sex addiction and has tools to use to turn this situation over to his Higher Power. The first thing that happens is John begins to worry and fret. The more he thinks about it, the more panic sets in. He starts feeling the urge to act out sexually. He begins to fantasize and then feels that familiar pulling - back toward active addiction. John begins to say the Serenity Prayer. He comes out of the trance he seems to be in and gets to a phone. He calls a person he knows that is home at that time. He tells the person about his potential problem of getting laid off from his job. The person on the other end of the line reminds John that what he has heard maybe only rumors and not fact. He also reminds John to repeat the Serenity Prayer, not to act out and to go to a meeting as soon as he can. John hangs up and is calmer. He doesn't act out. He knows that won't solve anything anyway. Later he attends a recovery meeting and the next day finds out that everything he heard was a rumor and wasn't even going to happen. Yes, it could have all been true and he may have been cut but regardless it would have just been an excuse to act out if he had. In this case John turned this situation over and didn't have to act out. These successes happen often as long as we stay focused on our recovery and work the program laid out in the steps. A Higher Power is caring for us by keeping us sober as we cooperate in sobriety. This is the beginning of a faith that works. This is the beginning of humility.

The phrase *to the care of God* as mentioned above comes when we turn things over to God. We are trusting that our Higher Power will take *care* of the results of our decisions in recovery. Sorry, getting a fancy car and lots of loot are not what we mean. What we do mean brings a richer experience, that if we cooperate in staying sober by taking action on our decisions (going to meetings and working the steps, etc.), then we have made decisions towards staying sexually sober and we trust God to care for us by keeping us sober. If we have developed a concept of a loving God then it stands to reason that this God will also care for us and for our decisions towards staying sober. After we've thought them through and acted upon them our Higher Power will take care of the results. The results we want are sobriety and peace of mind. In addition to discussing with our sponsor or other recovering people what we intend doing, we pray to our Higher Power about those intentions and we turn the results of our actions over to that power. We have turned things over to *the care of God*.

132

In a nutshell, in the 3rd Step we make a decision to simply work through the rest of the 12 Steps and to quit reacting to life's problems. We pray to our Higher Power for help and share with our support group. If we take care of our insides the outsides seem to take care of themselves. We make decisions about working our program and about getting into action to stay sober and we allow our Higher Power to handle the results of these decisions.

It may be beneficial to speak about *reacting to life's problems.* In the 3rd Step we stop reacting to problems. We, as sex addicts, tend to want to control everyone and everything around us instead of letting go and living life on life's terms. Instead of spending a lot of energy controlling everyone around us, we begin to allow God to change us (NOT OTHERS!) and we clean off our own side of the street. We attend to changing our own attitudes and we monitor ourselves to see if we are on track. We begin to develop our own space and we learn to live in it.

If we attend to our own attitude on a regular basis we will find peace and serenity. We will not be so interested in the other guy's faults and we will begin to see that, as a friend Bill A. used to say 'if I'm not the problem - there is no solution.'

After we have agreed on our own idea of a Higher Power in the previous step, we begin to concentrate in this step to utilize our newly found faith to stay sexually sober.

1) Do I have any reservations about turning my thoughts and decisions over to this power?

_____

_____

_____

_____

_____

2) Have I discussed the meaning of turning it over with my support group or my sponsor?

_____

_____

_____

_____

3) Am I willing to *act as if* God will take care of my sobriety when I work a program of recovery? (If we don't believe, we act *as if* we believe by doing the actions to stay sober and practice not worrying. If we act *as if* long enough, we may come to believe through our actions. We act our way into a new way of thinking).

_____

_____

_____

_____

_____

_____

○If we have a slip does this mean that God is not working in our recovery; that faith doesn't work? It may mean that we are not recovered enough to *not slip*. A person who is hit by a truck doesn't usually go to the hospital with multiple broken bones and leave the next day and run a marathon. It takes time for us to heal properly when we are beginning our recovery from sex addiction. We can use the slips we do have to learn more about ourselves as we recover.

4) Have I tended to lose faith quickly and become discouraged (past or present)? Explain.

_____

_____

_____

_____

5) Have I tried faith before and found it lacking? Describe your answer.

_____

_____

_____

_____

o Many of us, who have had faith in a Higher Power and who have lost our faith, have a difficult time trusting again. Accept that it may be hard to trust again, while at the same time staying open to the possibility.

6) Have I had faith and lost it. Am I now willing to believe that if it works for others that it could work for me? Explain.

_____

_____

_____

_____

7) Have I had an opportunity to practice turning a negative situation over to my Higher Power by using the tools of the program? Name two.

a) _____

_____

_____

b) _____

_____

_____

_____

8) Have I made a decision to work the rest of the 12 Steps?

_____

_____

_____

_____

9) Name three (recent) ways you have attempted to control other people's emotions or actions?

a) _____

_____

b) _____

_____

c) _____

_____

10) Have you tried monitoring your own emotions when conflicting with others? How.

_____

_____

_____

_____

11) Am I now willing to practice not reacting to negative situations in my life by using the tools of the program? What tools am I now using to stay in recovery?

_____

_____

_____

_____

Check the answers that best describe how you feel or what you think or what you experience about the following statements (double check any answers that you feel strongly about):

12) Many grow up in families that develop their own ideas about a Higher Power. Some grow up in strict religious families or in religious families who were not so strict. Others didn't have any religious or spiritual upbringing and some were taught to be against anything spiritual. In this step we look into spiritual matters but aren't concerned about religious belief.

____I was brought up atheist (against religion or the idea of God).

____I was brought up agnostic (didn't know one way or
the other).

____I was raised in a strict religious family.

____I was raised with religion and didn't have much
interest.

____I was interested in spiritual things but my parents weren't.

13) Some people are judgmental when it comes to spiritual matters and some aren't. Others don't really care one way or the other. Some don't believe in spirituality but are tolerant toward people who do.

____I don't care for those who have different ideas
than me about faith; I think they're all wrong.

___I try not to be judgmental with people of faith but I
   think they go to extremes at times.

___I am interested in finding something that works for
   me.

14) We, in recovery, are interested in developing a relationship with God as we understand God
    so that this power can keep us sober. We first have to develop a trust in God or we have to
    act as if we trust.

___I have a Higher Power that I am OK with and want to find out about turning my life
   over.

___I am fearful about spiritual matters and don't think I
   can turn my life over to God even though I worked Step 2.

___I am uncomfortable about turning my entire life over
   to my Higher Power. I want to control some things.

___I'm OK with my concept of God but I have reservations about giving my will over to
   God.

15) As recovering sex addicts, we make a decision while working Step 3 to work the remaining
    steps. At first some of us had reservations but when we completed our step work we
    discovered that we had tools to live a better life.

___ I am OK about working through the 12 Steps.

___ I don't know if the steps will work for me.

___ I would rather just go to meetings and not have to
   work the steps.

___ I have seen others stay sexually sober who have
   worked the steps and so I believe the steps will work
   for me.

16) Some people have difficulty making decisions. One may make a decision and see it through
    while another may go back and forth trying to make a decision or changing their minds
    about their decisions.

___I have difficulty sticking with my decisions.

___I can make a decision but question making it.

___I can make decisions without too many problems.

___I seem to struggle with making decisions and especially concerning sobriety.

17) There are many good examples of people staying sober who worked the steps. A shift seems to take place when they decide to work the program and accept responsibility for their recovery.

___I have seen people in the meetings who are progressing and they look different from when they came in.

___I have a desire to work the steps and change.

___I want what they have in the recovery meetings.

18) There are some things we want to hold on to and some we will let go of quickly. Control is one of the tough ones. We used sex to control our moods and other people.

___I have control issues when I want my way.

___I start controlling when things get crazy.

___I try to pray through rough situations in an attempt to give control to my Higher Power.

___I don't have many control issues.

19) Trust is sometimes difficult especially when we can't see our Higher Power. This is where faith comes in. We do the work and trust God to handle the results even when things don't look like they are working. We see our Higher Power by the results that take place. Don't quit five minutes before the miracle.
___When I see things going wrong I begin doubting my Higher Power.

___I am sometimes concerned when things don't look like they will be OK but I wait and see.

____When things start going wrong I call a member in my recovery meetings and we talk it over.

____I have seen God work in my life and I am OK about faith.

20) We begin to react less to life as we go further into recovery. The wild emotional roller-coaster slows down and we regain some balance.

____I feel really off balance so far.

____I can see the program working for me, I have calmed down somewhat.

____I am still experiencing the roller-coaster emotions.

____I am still acting out some and I get upset often.

The recovery meetings for sex addiction are a good place to hear examples of how to work Step 3. We share our concerns and we listen to the experience of the members who share. We attend the 'meeting before the meeting' (we get there early) and we attend the 'meeting after the meeting' (we stay after the meeting a few minutes and talk instead of leaving quickly after it ends). During the week we call others and we bookend.

Bookending is used formally in several 12 Step programs. Here is an example of bookending in recovery from sex addiction (developed by Debtors Anonymous): As soon as we have something stressful happen in our life we call someone in recovery. When we have handled the situation we call back and discuss what we did to resolve the problem or to calm our feelings about the problem. How does this help? It helps us to be accountable to someone in recovery and to ourselves to handle the situation rather than acting out compulsively. These actions help to stabilize us when we become off balance.

We use the first three steps of our recovery program as a basis for working the other nine steps. In the 1st Step *if* we keep acting out on our addictive circle behaviors, we will remain distracted by our disease and we won't possibly be able to work on any other step. If we don't work Step 2 and remind ourselves that we have a Higher Power that can and will return us to sanity from our insane thinking or behavior, we will be back to trying to stay sober on our own resources, using our own insane thoughts to steer us. Step 3 is the decision step.

The principle of Step 3 is: COMMITMENT.

We make a commitment (a decision to commit) to our Higher Power and to our program of recovery, and then we go about doing this by working the remaining 12 Steps.

I heard this in a meeting once: "God can't steer a parked car." What that meant to me was that I am required to drive the vehicle of my life by making decisions and acting on them. I gather all of the information I can and move forward. When I was a teenager learning to drive, my dad sat on one side as my teacher, and when I began to steer the vehicle into danger he would reach over and assist me to guide it back to safety. Similarly my Higher Power does the same thing for me in life. I make a decision and if it is leading to danger or if my decision is not good for me, God reaches over and steers me into a path that is more productive and right for me. Also heard in meetings: Make plans but don't plan the outcome. God determines outcomes contingent on our spiritual maintenance. We cooperate in our sobriety.

When we work the first two steps we become more stable. As we move into Step 3 we calm down and trust our Higher Power. This makes it easier as we move forward to start working the next step – Step 4.

Some of us recite this prayer illustrated below in the morning or before we start our day. We start out with the proper attitude of allowing our Higher Power to guide us and to direct our thinking. This reliance on our creator is the beginning of a life-long practice. We can't stay sober on our own power. Furthermore, there won't always be people around us who understand. So, in the end, our reliance must be on God..

The 3rd Step Prayer has been rewritten from the book Alcoholics Anonymous concerning Step 3. We now recite this prayer found on the next page (with our sponsor present we read):

3rd Step Prayer

God I give myself to you

To build with me and to do with me as you will.

Relieve me of the bondage of self

That I may better do your will.

Take away my difficulties that victory over them

May bear witness to those that I would help

Of your power, your love, and your way of life.

May I do your will always.

So Be It.

In Step 4 and 5 we begin the process of clearing away the debris on our insides to make room for God. Our character defects have caused confusion and have distracted us from being able to focus on doing God's will. God's will for me is to: Trust God, clean house, and help others. We begin next to work our 4th and 5th Step.

PART 3: THE HOUSE CLEANING STEPS:
Steps 4, 5, 6 & 7

KJ Nivin

STEPS 4 & 5

_____

145

CHAPTER 7

STEPS 4 & 5

Taking Inventory

STEP 4: Moral Inventory

We have done much work so far. We have created a stable base by working the first three steps. It is necessary to continue working the first three steps in order to keep us on track while we begin to process Step 4. The 4th Step through the 7th Step is used to deal with our insides. The 4th Step is written as: *Made a searching and fearless moral inventory of ourselves.*

The first question that comes to mind is: What is a moral inventory? A moral inventory is used to help discern what, inside us, leads us to act and think as we do, in ways that don't always produce positive or productive results. We find that there are patterns of thinking that we have developed that don't work for us anymore. We sometimes display defective thinking and our character suffers. We call these 'defects of character'. These defects of character cause us to take actions that harm ourselves and others. When we take an inventory of ourselves we sit down and write out who we have harmed and how we have harmed them. We then list the defects of character in each situation that caused us to react and to harm others.

As our inventory progresses we may find that we have been harmed as well. If we were harmed we also write down who was involved. The main focus still should be on the part we played and what defect of character caused us problems. It is essential in Step 4 that we take *our own inventory* and not inventory the faults of others.

Our basic problem, as sex addicts, is self-centered fear. It permeates everything in our life. We are either afraid of losing what we have or not getting what we want. When self-centered fear is triggered, it triggers character flaws that we have held onto for years. These flaws come out in some of the ways listed below.

List of Character Defects

Here is an *a to z* category list of character defects that you may consider, *check* the ones you identify with and double check the ones you strongly identify with:

a. Controlling, willful
b. Using denial
c. Disloyal or being loyal when it is not deserved
d. Egotistical, self important, conceited, arrogant (covert or overt)
e. Envious
f. Falsely proud, self- righteous, boastful
g. Fearful, projecting (negatively), worrying, untrusting
h. Gluttony
i. Gossiping, critical
j. Greedy, untrustworthy
k. Guilty (negative), self-condemning
l. Hateful, indifferent, revengeful, negative, unforgiving
m. Impatient
n. Irritable, resentful, argumentative, passive aggressive
o. Indolent
p. Jealous, possessive
q. Judgmental, condemning
r. Lustful
s. Lying, dishonest, manipulative, rationalizing, approval-seeking
t. People-pleasing, phony, saying yes when we mean no
u. Perfectionistic, prideful
v. Prejudiced, intolerant
w. Procrastinating, lazy, emotionally paralyzed
x. Self-pitying, full of self-hatred, depressive
y. Selfish, self-centered, self-seeking
z. Shameful

Looking at the example list above, we can see that character defects are negative attributes.. When we make an inventory it is wise also to list our good character traits on a list separate from our bad ones. As we seek balance, we keep in mind that all of us are a mixture of good and bad characteristics.

KJ Nivin

Here is an *a to z* category list of positive character traits, *check* the ones you identify with and double *check* the ones you strongly identify with:

a. Agreeable, Supportive
b. Calm, content
c. Cheerful
d. Consistent, confident, determined
e. Courageous, brave, assertive
f. Fair, just, forgiving
g. Faithful
h. Friendly, sharing
i. Generous, giving, helpful
j. Gentle, compassionate
k. Giving, kind, caring
l. Happy, positive
m. Honest (with self or others), ethical, moral
n. Hopeful
o. Humble, modest
p. Having integrity, honorable
q. Loving, considerate
r. Loyal (work, home, socially)
s. Non-judgmental
t. Optimistic, open minded
u. Patient
v. Proud (in a healthy sense)
w. Respectful
x. Responsible
y. Trusting (self or others)
z. willing

These lists of character traits above are limited. There are many more good and not so good traits. List other traits that you discover as you progress. You may have to research to find more. These are but a few examples that allow you to identify what is inside. From character traits listed above, look up synonyms for any of the words you strongly identify with. This will help you to become more familiar with them.

In our 4th Step we identify the good traits and keep them. We search out the character flaws and in a later step we ask our Higher Power to remove them. We may sometimes act out our negative character flaws, sometimes in moderation and other times to extremes, causing us difficulty interacting with others.

149

In this section your answers may be more brief and there is room for notes on the side. Ask yourself the following questions:

1) What are four of my most valuable character traits?

   a) _____

   b) _____

   c) _____

   d) _____

2) Name four of your worst character defects (traits).

   a) _____

   b) _____

   c) _____

   d) _____

3) Did you find it easier to name your good traits or the bad traits?. Explain.

   _____

   _____

   _____

   _____

4) Do you consider some of the negative traits on the list as good or useful traits? Which ones and why?

   a) _____

   _____

150

b) _____

_____

c) _____

_____

5) Is there anyone in your family of origin that has the same or similar character traits as you (positive or negative). Name the person (s) and the trait(s).

_____

_____

_____

_____

6) Do you have or have you had a good relationship with the people identified in the previous question? Explain.

_____

_____

_____

_____

7) Are there character traits that you are proud of? Name two or more.

a) _____

_____

b) _____

_____

8) Are there character traits you are ashamed of?

a) _____

_____

b) _____

_____

9) If you had your choice, which character flaws would you like *not to* be part of your life. Name three. Why not?

a) _____

_____

_____

b) _____

_____

_____

c) _____

_____

_____

10) Do you think you have none or very few character flaws or do you think you have many? Explain.

_____

_____

_____

_____

_____

_____

11) Focusing on positive traits, do you think you have only a few good character traits? Explain.

_____

_____

_____

_____

_____

_____

12) Do I experience self-centered fears (fear of losing what you have or not getting what you want)? What are they and how do they show up in your life today?

_____

_____

_____

_____

_____

13) Have I experienced abandonment or the fear of abandonment now or in my past? Explain.

_____

_____

_____

_____

_____

14) Are there beliefs that I have that don't go along with my new way of life (spiritual life or recovery)? Explain.

_____

_____

_____

_____

_____

15) Do I have prejudice against a race, ideals, concepts etc. (people, places or things) that I am willing to reconsider?

_____

_____

_____

_____

_____

16) Do you suffer self-hatred? Do you physically strike or abuse yourself? List all ways in which either of these are true.

_____

_____

_____

In the 4th Step we make a list of those we have harmed with sex or any other way. We list our resentments, fears and shame and briefly describe what happened. We consider these questions: "Have you harmed other individuals or institutions? Were you harmed by any individuals, institutions, or organizations?" We write down who we had problems with and what happened. If we don't remember names we write out and describe the incident anyway. Was there money involved that was stolen or misused by you or from you? Am I angry with my Higher Power or with myself? Think of these questions when you begin your inventory below.

Taking a Moral Inventory

When we list all people and institutions we have done harm to and that have harmed us, we list even the small ways we were involved. Your list may be extensive because it will span a lifetime. *Start from earliest memories.* Some recovering addicts have experienced resentment and hurt in their present life that stem from sensitivity born in childhood experiences. A parent, other relatives, a friend, or stranger may have been involved. Memories may pop up randomly. So, make a habit of jotting down a word or two as a reminder if you are in the middle of doing something else. We want to be sure and capture anything that our mind offers up. *We list everything from our past to our present that bothers us.* We inventory our thoughts about ourselves. Is there self-hatred or self-pity? Do we fancy ourselves as better than others? Do we have low self-esteem?

Our main goal in this part of the process of recovery is not to assign blame. Rather, it is to understand our part while identifying our character defects. We will use this information in later steps. Our inventory may take several weeks to complete but we should not drag our feet. As a rule of thumb, we check in with our sponsors throughout writing our 4th Step and allow input from them and other recovering sex addicts who have completed this step.

Use the format below for your inventory (it is suggested to use one page for each issue).

Example:
List my shame/guilt   *I am ashamed that I missed my son's school play because I was acting out. It hurt him and angered my spouse. I have done this on several other occasions.*

How did (do) I react to it? *I reacted with anger towards my wife when she questioned me about it. I couldn't look into my son's eyes. Our friends knew that something was wrong but I made up excuses.* (May be longer explanation)

Defects triggered: *The defects triggered were lying, anger, defensiveness, guilt, shame and denial.*

What could I have done or can I do differently? *I could have owned up to my problem with sex? Now that I am recovering I can monitor my defensiveness when my wife wants to know my whereabouts.* (May be longer explanation)

The following pages provide sample sheets to help you process your 4th step work. You may require more sheets than are provided. For guidance in writing your inventory, refer to the *a to z list* of character defects in Chapter 7:

List my shame guilt

_____

_____

_____

_____

_____

How did (do) I react to it?

_____

_____

_____

_____

Defects triggered

What could I have done or can I do differently?

I am resentful at (people, places, or things)

What was (is) my part in it?

Defects triggered

What could I have done or can I do differently?

I am fearful of (people, places, or things)

_____

_____

_____

_____

How did (does) it affect me?

_____

_____

_____

_____

Defects triggered

_____

_____

_____

_____

What could I have done or can I do differently?

_____

_____

_____

_____

_____

_____

_____

_____

Harm I've done (people, places, or things) include sexual and non-sexual conduct

_____

_____

_____

_____

What was (is) my part in it?

_____

_____

_____

_____

Defects triggered

_____

_____

_____

_____

What could I have done or can I do differently?

_____

_____

_____

_____

_____

_____

_____

_____

<u>*Harm done to me (by people, places, things or by myself). Include sexual and non-sexual*</u>

_____

_____

_____

_____

<u>*What was (is) my part in it?*</u>

_____

_____

_____

_____

Defects triggered

_____

_____

_____

_____

What could I have done or can I do differently?

_____

_____

_____

_____

_____

_____

_____

Step 4 Inventory CheckList

After completing your inventory place a check mark by the statements that are true for you past or present or partially true (circle the part that is true for you) and ask yourself this question: Did I leave any of these off my inventory list?

_____ Did I place on my 4th Step all embarrassing or degrading situations that I am ashamed of?

____ Have I left off anything that should go on my list of harm I've caused?

____ Have I justified leaving any person or institution off my inventory because they have harmed me more?

____ Did I take money and find I don't want to pay it back?

____ Am I ashamed to include harm done to me because the nature of the incident was embarrassing?

____ Have I left off anything that should go on my list of harm I've caused because I don't think I hurt those involved that badly?

____ Did I list stolen work time as harm caused by me (surfing the net, flirting, acting out on the job, leaving the job to act out or just goof off, etc.)?

____ Am I being honest with myself and my sponsor about my inventory?

____ Have I shared in meetings and with recovering sex addicts about the experience of writing a 4th Step?

____ Have I taken items from work, church, or other organizations I am associated with (copy paper, pens, petty cash or other small items)?

____ Are there people, places or things in my past that I don't remember so well and have conveniently left off my inventory?

____ Is there an incident (s) where I don't know names of people involved but I remember the incident well?

____ Were there sexual problems in my family of origin that I have left out?

____ Did I put resentments or self-abuse issues on my inventory (slapping, hitting, cutting self, or hatred or anger with self, sexual abuse of self with objects or devices)?

____ Did I put resentments or other negative feelings I have about my Higher Power?

____ Have I been harmed by clergy, staff, or institution members and wish not to put this on my list?

____ Did I have any consensual sexual contact (touching or sexual in nature) with an adult or someone older than me when I was young?

____ Am I attempting to protect someone by leaving them off my list?

____ Did any childhood sexual contact include aunt, uncle, brother, sister, mother, father, grandparent, stepparent, cousin, relative, stepbrother or -sister, etc.?

____ Was there anyone that made sexual comments – degrading or complimentary-- towards me or about my body during my childhood?

____ Are there any fuzzy childhood memories about babysitters, neighbors or anyone living near you involving sexual contact with you?

____ Have I had sexual problems with my own children, stepchildren or any child?

____ Have I participated in any voyeuristic behaviors (looking out my window into neighbors windows, waiting near women's dressing rooms to get a peak, around stairwells, up skirts, down blouses etc.) that need to go on my list?

____ Have I walked in front of my home windows to expose myself?(Covertly or overtly).

____ Have I dressed or positioned myself in sexual ways in an attempt to attract others?

____ Have I prostituted myself as a child or as an adult?

____ Did I have sexual contact with professional counselors or doctors?

____ Have I asked my family of origin about any possible sexual problems during childhood? This step work may be the first safe place we have had to look at our lives honestly. So, take the risk and do so here. Now go back to your inventory and add the items you left off.

Make an appointment to present your 5th Step, but don't present it before working the material in the next chapter. Merely set a date so that you can eliminate procrastination.

It is time for a break. You deserve it. Take a Serenity Break and relax a moment:

After going through your relaxation process, review, in your mind, what you've accomplished so far, how things were when you started recovery and what it is like for you now after doing this work. You are not finished but you have digested much. Keep up the good work. You display much courage working through the 12 Steps. Give yourself, your sponsor, your support system and your Higher Power credit. We become co-creators with God as we understand God. What are we creating? We are creating a new life for ourselves, a life of success, a sober life. Our new life can include anything we choose: healthy relationships, peace of mind, serenity, and a life worth living. It works if we work it. Keep coming back.

The principle of Step 4 is: HONESTY.

After our program check we take a break for a few days but not over a week so we can digest and process the work we've done so far. After our few days *centering break* we move on to the next step, Step 5.

_____

Program Check

So far you have added more actions to your program of sobriety; tools that work:

You are going to at least one meeting a week and/or receiving help with your addiction to sex and you now have a home group.

You know who your sponsor is and are working with him or her on the 12 Steps.

You have a few phone numbers of members of your sexual recovery group and are making phone calls on a regular basis.

You are reading sexual addition oriented recovery material and a meditation book

You are journaling or writing a weekly stressor list and you are making mental notes of your feelings, you are making daily sobriety plans to get through the day without acting out and you are using your circles.

You may be over physical or emotional withdrawal or know how to deal with it better.

Q. Are you practicing not reacting to negative situations and people? (Yes)   (No)

165

Q. Are you relying on your Higher Power more and are you abstinent from sexually acting out?
(Yes)   (No)

KJ Nivin

STEP 5: Admitted Our Wrongs

We look at the 5th Step as a tool to complete the work done in the last step. Step 4 has prepared us for this new process by giving us a written inventory about who we are and what we've done in more detail than when we presented our first step. We are now ready to talk these details over with our sponsor. This is Step 5: *Admitted to God, to ourselves, and to another human being (our sponsor) the exact nature of our wrongs.*

Defining Step 5

In breaking this step down, the word *admitted* is fairly straight forward. We tell another person (our sponsor) exactly what we did and who we hurt (our wrongs). What does it mean that we admitted to ourselves and to God these wrongs?

In doing our inventory and by writing it down we admitted to ourselves the wrongs we did. It took great integrity to concede that we had done far more wrong than we previously admitted. Thus, in essence we have admitted to ourselves our wrongs. We may want to re-read our 4th Step as preparation for presenting it to our sponsor, but we need to be sure we don't change things so as to make them not seem so bad. This re-reading or of our 4th Step may help us admit our wrongs to ourselves.

To admit our wrongs to our Higher Power, God as we understand God, can be done in several ways. We may believe that God knows everything about us. If so, what's to hide?. Why should we worry about admitting our wrongs to God when God seems to be all knowing? Why be rigorously honest when there is truly nothing we can hide from God?

Some consider that writing and presenting their 5th Step to their sponsors is all they need to do to admit their wrongs to God.. Others write a letter to God and ask for forgiveness and ask their Higher Power to help them do better in the future. Some use the technique of placing a chair in front of them and imagine that their Higher Power is sitting there. They proceed to read their 4th step inventory aloud. This may sound silly but some report they have had the feeling of the presence of God while doing so. Some have wept and laughed as they read aloud. Reading it aloud has helped them to hear it themselves. There is no hard and fast rule on how to admit to God our wrongs. You may come up with your own ideas of what is best for you.. The important thing is that we make an appointment with our sponsor and complete this step by discussing our wrongs and by listening to feedback that is given. By doing this we are practicing letting go of control and of our old ideas.

When we make an appointment with our sponsor to present our 5th Step we need to insure that we have ample, uninterrupted time to complete this step. It is possible that this presentation can take six to eight hours to complete. It may have to be done in several sessions. The important thing is to be in a place that is free of phone calls or other interruptions.

We discuss, with our sponsor, how we felt in each instance of wrongdoing. We also discuss any money we mishandled. We admit each defect of character we displayed in each situation and we expand this discussion of that particular character defect so as to get the full impact of our part in the problem. We cease blaming anything or anyone for our wrongs. Yes, we weren't entirely wrong in each instance, but maybe when we were wronged by others we harbored resentments toward them and sought revenge by gossip or by other actions.

Whatever the situation with individuals or institutions/organizations (churches, governments, work, societies, sects, politics or anything you may add to this list) we talk over with our sponsor and allow ourselves to experience our feelings as they happen.

Answer the following questions below:

1) Do I have reservations (fears) about doing my 5th Step? Monitor your gut feelings and write these down. Am I nervous, fearful of change etc.?

_____

_____

_____

_____

_____

2) Are there defects of character that I don't want to admit or fear that if I do admit to them that I will have to stop using them?

_____

_____

_____

_____

_____

3) Are there specific issues that you do not wish to discuss with others and that you want to take to the grave with you? List them here and explain.

a) _____

_____

_____

_____

_____

_____

_____

b) _____

_____

_____

_____

_____

_____

_____

4) Are you holding back making an appointment with your sponsor to present your 5th Step? Why?

_____

_____

_____

_____

_____

_____

5) Have you spoken with others who have completed their Step 5 and asked for feedback? What did they offer as guidance?

_____

_____

_____

_____

_____

o You may want to share your feelings or reservations about this process in your recovery meeting. We are only as sick as our secrets. There is stress associated with working this step so insure you maintain your balance and stay free from acting out on your addictive circle behaviors. It is also wise to stay out of your ritual circle so as not to trigger your sexual compulsion.

6) Am I still using, to the best of my ability, the tools of recovery to help me work this step? List the tools you are now using.

_____

_____

_____

_____

_____

_____

7) Do I have shame or guilt associated with telling another human being? Explain.

_____

_____

_____

_____

_____

8) Have I read recovery literature and other sources to get perspective on the 5th Step?

_____

_____

_____

_____

9) Does your family know generally about your 12 step work? Are they supportive?

_____

_____

_____

_____

_____

_____

10) Is there a lot of chaos or turmoil going on in your life as you approach completing this step? Is this holding you back in completing this step?

_____

_____

_____

_____

_____

_____

11) Name three reasons it would help your life to complete your 5th Step. What are the benefits?

a) _____

_____

_____

_____

b) _____

_____

_____

_____

c) _____

   _____

   _____

   _____

12) Do I wonder why I must share my 5th Step and am I fearful of having to discuss it with another person?

_____

_____

_____

_____

_____

_____

13) Have I had to reschedule presenting my Step 5 once or more? This may be due to procrastination. Explain. If not, explain the arrangements you have made.

_____

_____

_____

_____

_____

_____

14) Have I arranged my schedule to accommodate presenting this step?

_____

_____

_____

_____

_____

_____

Presenting the 5th Step

We make our appointment with our sponsor and go to it. Be sure that you and your sponsor's schedule accommodate giving your 5th Step presentation in part or in full and that it is uninterrupted. If you can't finish it in one sitting make another appointment to complete it and follow through. It is suggested that you make notes on a note pad or on your inventory pages of the harm (or "THE WRONGS") done that you hadn't included on your inventory. Also make note of new information you discover during your discussion with your sponsor.

The principle of Step 5 is: TRUTH.

Our main goal in Step 5 is to tell the truth about our disease. We tell on our 'addict' within. We identify our character defects that have for so long influenced our life and relationships. We begin to separate from our addict. We find out who we are and who the addict within is.

The scary part was over when we presented our 1st Step. So relax. The 5th Step is, in part, a continuation of that 1st Step process. We use Step 5 when working Steps 7 through 9. We are beginning to let go of the past: our past hurts, fears, shame, guilt and other negative feelings that keep us stuck. Easy does it, but do it. We are moving forward. This step helps free us from the past. We do not regret the past nor wish to shut the door on it. This is our hope in Step 4 through Step 9.

After completing Step 5 we now look at Step 6 and Step 7.

STEPS 6 & 7

_____

Process of Sexual Recovery

CHAPTER 8

STEPS 6 & 7

Facing Our Defects

STEP 6: *Were Entirely Ready*

Were entirely ready to have God remove all these defects of character is Step 6. This step, along with the next step, is considered in some fellowships to be the step that separates the men from the boys and the women from the girls. In other words, in working through this process, it shows that we are becoming more mature in our growth.

The character defects we identified and discussed in the previous steps are now placed on a separate list called our 6th Step list. We use Step 6 to mentally and emotionally prepare ourselves to be rid of our character flaws. Some of us have tried to hold on to these old ideas but found that there were no results until we let go completely. Remember that we deal with sexual compulsion/addiction; it's cunning, baffling and powerful.

Step 6 Defined

Many of us feel that we have our entire lives shot through with character flaws. We have set up a system in which we rely upon these negative traits in order just to operate from day-to-day. What would happen if we decided to stop operating in and through this negative system? Would our lives collapse in on us? Can we imagine being honest on a minute-to-minute basis? Would it be practical to stop telling those little white lies that seem to make some things that seem really negative look better on the surface? How can we stop our anger? Wouldn't we become doormats? There are many more questions that come to mind when we consider *not* using our character defects to arrange things (manipulate) so that they go our way. Wouldn't we need something to fill the gap if we were seriously considering doing away with these handy, but defective tools? The answer is yes. We would have to use other methods to fill in for those discarded character traits. At this point in the process of working the steps however, we only need to be *ready* (entirely ready) to have them removed.

Just how do we become entirely ready? First we look at the facts. Our lives have been spiraling downward because of our sexual addiction. Our sexual addiction was out of our control to stop or to stay stopped and it was ruining our relationships and our lives. It triggered our character defects in extreme ways and we embodied them in harmful actions. Our character defects (defective thoughts and behaviors) fueled our sexual addiction by keeping us off balance and spiraling us back to active addiction. This became a vicious cycle. This caused us to hit bottom and seek help. These are the facts of our addiction. A life run on these patterns of behavior and thinking is a life destined for failure. We saw this truth when we presented our 1st Step. Is it so hard to admit that our way didn't work well and that we had need for some new input; that we needed to change?

Armed with this knowledge we became entirely willing to have God remove all our defects of character. We realize if we keep this flawed thinking in place that we set ourselves up for failure. If we decide to build a high wall in our back yard and we use good, sturdy brick for the top and middle but we use sand for our base, the wall will probably collapse. The same holds true for our program. To stay sexually sober we need to rid ourselves of the foundation of sand (our negative character defects) and build a more sturdy foundation based on good character. Our good character will support our recovery and not awaken the addict within, out of its slumber. We want to establish balance in our lives to make permanent recovery possible.

Step 6 List

1) Make a 6th Step list of *your undesirable* character defects. You may look back to the 4th and 5th Steps and use the character flaws you discovered there to compile your list below. You may also refer to Chapter 7 in this workbook as well. Write your own short definition after each character flaw.

a) _____

_____

b) _____

_____

c) _____

_____

d) _____

e) _____

f) _____

g) _____

h) _____

i) _____

j) _____

k) _____

l) _____

2) Now go back to question one and place check-marks on the character defects that you are <u>entirely ready</u> to have God remove.

3) In the first question, circle the defects that you are unwilling to give up yet.

32) Do I believe that I need to base my recovery on good character traits? Am I still holding onto the idea that I may not have to give up all my character defects? Give examples.

_____

_____

_____

_____

_____

_____

33) Do I have character defects that I use day-to-day and cringe when I think of giving them up (lying, fibbing, manipulation, people pleasing, worrying etc.)?

_____

_____

_____

_____

_____

34) Would I feel lost if I gave up the use of <u>all</u> of my old negative ways of thinking? Explain.

_____

_____

_____

_____

_____

_____

35) Is there some personal flawed thinking that I don't want to give up? Example: All men are jerks. Women are crazy. (Buzz phrases)

_____

_____

_____

_____

_____

_____

36) Do I believe that all I need is control to stopping my character defects?

_____

_____

_____

_____

_____

_____

37) Do I see other recovering sex addicts who have positive spiritual and emotional attributes that I would like to have for myself?

_____

_____

_____

_____

_____

_____

38) Name five attributes you would like to have more of.

_____

_____

_____

_____

_____

39) Name five character defects (negative traits) that you believe you have and would like to be rid of above any other; those that cause the most negative results.

_____

_____

_____

_____

_____

Assignment: **Take your list of character defects and transfer them onto a note card or small piece of paper that you can carry with you. Make a check when these flaws become active in your life during the week, repeat this weekly. Example:**

√√√	**Lied**
√√√√√	**Resentful**
√√√√	**Judgmental**
√√	**People pleased: said yes when I meant no**
√√√√√√√	**Manipulated others**

List all your faults as above and do this exercise weekly. Make notes in your journal at night of what was most troublesome for you.

As sex addicts we tend to hold on to things that are familiar to us even though they cause us great pain. These character defects have probably been with us all our lives; we are very familiar with them. There is a saying in the rooms of recovery that states: Pain is inevitable; *misery* is optional. When we hold on to these character defects and operate out of and through them we become miserable. When we let go of these defects it is often painful at first but our misery subsides. It is just like having a toothache. When we live with the aching tooth it is miserable, but when we summon up our courage and have the tooth pulled or repaired it is painful at first, but with healing the pain subsides.

The principle of Step 6 is: WILLINGNESS

Our goal here is to let go of our old ways and develop new ways to think and behavior. In doing so we cooperate with our Higher Power. *This power allows situations to arise that will let us practice the opposite character trait.* If we were weight lifters and we only practiced lifting very light weights we probably wouldn't increase in strength. We need to add more weight to our lifting in order to gain strength. Once we get used to that weight we add more to gain more strength. If we are placed in areas of growth in our lives that may be uncomfortable for us but that eventually will challenge us to change, we will be strengthened spiritually and emotionally once we get used to it. This is the work of our Higher Power. God adds the additional weights.

To work this step of becoming willing to have all our defects removed we talk in meetings, on the phone and with our sponsors. We pray and meditate on willingness. We focus our energies on what internal changes we need to make so that we can have that willingness. Think about how it was before recovery and how it is now and ask this question: Do I want to go back to that misery of being out of control and living in chaos? If the answer is *no* then we may be motivated enough to move on to Step 7. Practice this meditation provided as a Serenity Break.

Meditation

"I didn't know how to tell people that I was crazy."

In our Twelve Step Fellowships we enjoy communication with one another at emotional levels that are seldom felt in other areas of our lives.

Each and every member carries their own message of hope each time they share in their own *"unique mental dialect"*.

Before reaching our Fellowships, we may very well have been the "exceptions' to the

ordinary life experience felt by so-called "normal people".

Thankfully, upon entering our Fellowships we <u>soon</u> take on a radically different view of the old "status quo".

We soon begin learning that the "extraordinary"

problems we've lived with have real names. We

learn that the thoughts and feelings we were so sure

no one else ever had often proved to be rules

rather than exceptions among our new

recovering friends. We learned that we or no one else was

"terminally unique."

Written by a Recovering-12 Step Fellowship Member Lee E.

STEP 7 - *Humbly Asked*

We are now at Step 7. This is a critical step and we work this step just the way it is written: *Humbly asked God to remove all our shortcomings* (character defects). This step helps us work the next two steps so we pay particular attention to this process.

We arrived at the 7th Step by working the six previous steps. With each step building upon another, we work each step as if our very lives depended on it. And so it does. If we wanted to live free of our sexual acting out we needed to toe the line; we need to step up. As we stated before, this is the *working* part of the program. We go to meetings and fellowship with others but in this step we have to do the soul searching ourselves. This step is a continuation of the previous step. We put our willingness into action. We are now ready to have God remove all our character defects and we do so by humbly asking. We have made a list in Step 6 of our defects of character from the 4th and 5th Step process. Now we focus on completing this process with a prayer for God's help in relieving us of our shortcomings (character defects or character flaws).

We examine our 6th Step list of character defects. We use the prayer below to humbly ask God to remove all these character defects but in God's own time and on God's own terms. Don't expect all of your character defects to be removed in an instant. Some may fall away quickly while others remain. It took time to acquire them and it will take time to be rid of them. We thank God for what He gives us, what He takes away, and what He leaves us.

We find a place where we can be alone and undisturbed for an hour. We think back to the previous steps or we may review our workbook . Have we left anything out? Is there anything we are holding back from our sponsor? We meditate on this. If we have left something out we call or contact our sponsor and make our confession. This hour is used for straightening anything out that needs addressing. We think well before saying our prayer. If we are satisfied that we have not left anything out we proceed.

We sit quietly and go through our relaxation technique we learned and practiced previously. We calm our mind and body. As we begin to calm down we find stillness inside. Then we recite the prayer offered next:

7th Step Prayer

God

I give you all of me, good and bad, to you. I ask that from this point on that you guide me to better do your will. I ask that you now remove from me every defect of character that would get in the way of doing your will. I humbly ask that you do this in your own way and in your own time. As I go from here please guide me always. Your will be done.

Amen.

We bookend with our sponsor or someone in our recovery group and let them know we have completed our 7th Step. Remember that we seek change: If nothing changes – nothing changes.

In the following exercise concerning character, since we have our defects of character list from Step 6, let us also make a list of character traits that are worthwhile to us.

Desirable Character Trait List

1) Make a list of *your desirable* character traits below. These traits are the ones that you want in place of your character defects. You may look back to the 4th and 5th Steps and use the positive character traits you discovered in Chapter 7 *a to z* list to compile your list below. Write your own short definition after each positive character trait.

a) _____

_____

b) _____

_____

c) _____

d) _____

e) _____

f) _____

g) _____

h) _____

i) _____

j) _____

k) _____

l) _____

Assignment: **Take your list of good character traits and transfer them onto a note card or small piece of paper, as you did in Step 6. Set opposite, the character defect you wish to replace and carry this list with you. Make a check-mark (use pencil or erasable ink) when your character flaws or your good character traits become operative in your life during the week. Example:**

√√	**Lied**	√√√√√√**Was truthful**
√	**Resentment**	√√√√ **Was considerate**
√√	**Judgmental**	√√√**Was non-judgmental**
√√√	**People pleased**	√√ **True to self: said no when I meant no**
√√	**Manipulated**	√√√√**Set boundaries, was up front**

List all your good and bad character traits as above and do this exercise weekly. Make notes in your journal at night of what was most troublesome and what was most successful that day. If practiced, this exercise will aid you in replacing negative traits with positive ones. Remember that God ultimately has rein over *when and how* they are removed. God adds the weights.

After completing the assignment above, go back to question one and place checks on the positive character traits that you are presently using and that have taken the place of character defects.

Do I now believe that God will remove my defects of character?

The principle of Step 7 is: HUMILITY

We have now completed Step 7 process. If we practice this step on a regular basis, especially when we have defects of character that seem unmovable, we will find that, in time, God will remove these shortcomings and replace them with something better (our good character traits that we all possess but sometimes are not aware of) if we pray and ask God to remove our flawed traits. With our cooperation in being willing to change, we will be on our way to a life that works. We are now becoming God conscious and we are now beginning to rely more on God and less on our own thinking. We are gaining true humility. We are becoming *God centered.*

Program Check

You have added more actions to your program of sobriety:

You know who your sponsor is and are working with him or her on the 12 Steps and you have phone numbers of members in recovery and are making phone calls.

You are reading recovery literature and the meditation book *Answers in the Heart* on a regular basis.

You are journaling or writing a weekly stressor list, you are making mental note of your feelings and you are making daily sobriety plans to get through the day without acting out and you are using the circles.

You no longer have physical or emotional withdrawal or you know how to deal with it better.

You are practicing not reacting to negative situations and people and you are relying on your Higher Power more.

You are abstinent from your addictive circle behaviors and you feel more stable.

Q. Have you shared your concerns with your support group or your sponsor? (Yes) or (No)

Q. Did you make a list of good and bad traits on a note card and check them during the week? (Yes) or (No)

Q. Have you completed the first seven steps in a way that satisfies you?   (Yes) or (No)

We move on to Step 8.

PART 4: THE AMENDS STEPS
Steps 8 & 9

Process of Sexual Recovery

196

STEPS 8 & 9

Process of Sexual Recovery

CHAPTER 9

STEPS 8 & 9

Making Amends

STEP 8: Made a list

In this step we begin the process of amends. We compile a list of people and institutions / organizations we have harmed and we discuss them with our support group and our sponsor. Step 8 is written as: *Made a list of all persons we had harmed and became willing to make amends to them all.*

Where do we get this list of people? In our 4th Step we listed people we had harmed. This list should include anyone, even institutions or organizations that we have dealt with in a less than loving or honest way. In our 5th Step we discussed how we have wronged others and whom we have wronged.

Step 8 List

We make our 8th Step list and then go through the process of becoming willing to straighten out our past. Is this a tall order? Yes it is, but this step and the next one is part of the process of letting go of the past's control over us. In order for us, as recovering sex addicts, to have lasting sobriety, we have to go to any length. Just how far do we go? We need to keep in mind this step deals only with making a list and becoming willing. If we jump ahead with concerns about actually facing those we have wronged, we are not taking it one step at a time. We are projecting fears and concerns into the future that embody two acronyms for F.E.A.R: False Expectations Appearing Real and Forget Everything and Run. In this 8th Step, we simply make our list and Face Everything and Recover.

1) Go back to your written 4th Step inventory and to your Step 5 notes (if any) and begin the process of listing everyone (people, places and things) you have harmed (physically,

emotionally or spiritually, financially or in other ways). You may use the space below to list them and to make a short note of what happened and what amend you feel you owe. Example:

Julie - used her for sex only. Amends: Need to stay away.

Joe's Pizza - stole money from table. Amends: Admitted to the owner that you stole tip money in the past and replenish the money with interest.

Work - padded expense account and missed work to go have sex. Amends: Work additional hours to pay this back, stop missing work, stop stealing, and stop acting out.

John - resented him for informing my wife about an affair with his wife. Amends: Stay away from John and his wife and pray for them or in time, *if practical*, go to John (with support) and admit my part in the affair with his wife, and for resenting him for telling wife (**It is wise to seek counseling before proceeding**).

Childhood acquaintance - molested me, I hated her. Amends: Pray for this person daily and eventually consider confronting her after consulting my support group and counselor.

Job – Was fired from my previous company for looking at Internet porn and I resent them and I feel shame. Amends: Make appropriate amends by admitting to my boss what I have done was wrong and admit any harm done to the company. Pray for him/them.

Self and family – Admit my wrongs (amends) to them and continue working the steps and staying in recovery. Show love and patience and be present with them emotionally.

    With our entire list we pray for *willingness* to make these amends. We now make our list. In the next step we think of how we can make these amends. For now we just have to become willing.

a) _____

_____

_____

_____

b) _____

_____

_____

_____

c) _____

_____

_____

_____

d) _____

_____

_____

_____

e) _____

_____

_____

_____

f) _____

_____

_____

_____

g) _____

_____

_____

_____

h) _____

_____

_____

_____

i) _____

_____

_____

_____

j) _____

_____

_____

_____

k) _____

_____

_____

_____

l) _____

_____

_____

_____

m) _____

_____

_____

_____

n) _____

_____

_____

_____

o) _____

_____

_____

_____

p) _____

_____

_____

_____

q) _____

_____

_____

_____

r) _____

_____

_____

_____

s) _____

_____

_____

_____

t) _____

_____

_____

_____

u) _____

_____

_____

_____

v) _____

_____

_____

_____

w) _____

_____

_____

_____

x) _____

_____

_____

_____

y) _____

_____

_____

_____

z) _____

_____

_____

_____

_____

2) Going back to question number one, place a check-mark on the amends you owe that you are willing to make. (Remember that we are only dealing with the *willingness* to make the amends. We are not going out to make any amends at this time).

If any more space is needed, add more. How long should the list be? Some have reported that their list contained over 50 entries. We don't have to concern ourselves about the quantity, but we do need to concentrate on the quality. We place on our list those who we believe we owe amends. When we discuss this list with our sponsor. With guidance some may be eliminated or more may be added.

During this process we need input from other recovering sex addicts who have worked this step. They may be able to shed some light on any questions or reservations you may have about completing this list. Obviously if you ask people who have not done an 8th Step, you will get only an opinion from that person without the benefit of experience. It is best to seek out people who are recovering sex addicts and have completed this work themselves.

3) Are there any amends we owe that we have left off our list because of fear or justification?

_____

_____

_____

_____

_____

4) Have I discussed this step with my support system? Explain why or why not.

_____

_____

_____

_____

_____

5) Am I projecting into the future to the next step of making amends? Does this stop me from being entirely honest about my list of amends? Explain.

_____

_____

_____

_____

_____

_____

6) Name four fears I have in making my list of amends.

a) _____

_____

_____

b) _____

_____

_____

c) _____

_____

_____

d) _____

_____

_____

7) Were there STDs involved?

_____

_____

_____

_____

_____

8) Were there other embarrassing issues that need to be discussed?

_____

_____

_____

_____

_____

9) Is there anyone on your amends list above who need to be added or taken off the list? (This should be discussed with a sponsor.)

_____

_____

_____

_____

_____

On a scale of one to ten, circle the number representing how you feel or think about the following statements (one being slight and ten being intense):

Fear of writing down all people I have harmed.

1____2____3____4____5____6____7____8____9____10

Angry with those who have harmed me

1____2____3____4____5____6____7____8____9____10

Projection of negative results into the future

1____2____3____4____5____6____7____8____9____10

Trust in my Higher Power to help me becoming willing to make amends.

1____2____3____4____5____6____7____8____9____10

Confidence I have listed all my amends

1____2____3____4____5____6____7____8____9____10

I have looked for input from others for help concerning my amends.

1____2____3____4____5____6____7____8____9____10

Having anxiety about making amends

1____2____3____4____5____6____7____8____9____10

I have shared in my support group / meeting about making amends

1____2____3____4____5____6____7____8____9____10

I have prayed for willingness

1____2____3____4____5____6____7____8____9____10

I have used Serenity Breaks to calm and rest myself regularly.

1____2____3____4____5____6____7____8____9____10

I have used the Serenity Prayer day by day.

1____2____3____4____5____6____7____8____9____10

I have stayed away from addictive and ritual circle behaviors

1____2____3____4____5____6____7____8____9____10

I believe that I am willing to make amends to all I have harmed

1____2____3____4____5____6____7____8____9____10

If we are thorough and prayerful about this 8th Step we will begin to surrender to our Higher Power and become willing to make all of our amends.

The principle of Step 8 is: REFLECTION

We reflect on our relationships with others and we decide to take action and repair the damage we have caused or were a part of.

We work this step by taking our list and praying for our Higher Power's will in each instance. This will help prepare us for our 9th Step amends. We pray for willingness to make amends as opportunities present themselves. We want to keep in mind that these are our amends to the people and places on our list. Thus, we pray that God remove any anger and other negative feelings we may have towards that person, institution or principle. These negative feelings will get in our way of making proper amends.

We discuss this with our sponsor and others in recovery until we have willingness. It may be best to start out with praying about the lesser amends first (amends that are smaller in importance) and then move on to the more hurtful and fearful ones. We may have been harmed also but if we hold grudges or resentments (spiritually damaging) we pray to be free of these feelings. We will need to make amends later in the 9th Step for harm done by us. This is the next step in our progress. Before proceeding to Step 9 and after talking with your sponsor about any reservations you may have about being willing to make all amends you owe, recite this prayer (in your own words or as written) and afterward take a few days *centering break*:

8th Step Willingness Prayer

God

I have listed harm done to myself, to others, and you. Please help me with the willingness to make all my amends great and small. Help me to humble myself and to admit my wrongs to others. Give me the grace to be honest and open. Help me to receive your grace.

Your will be done.

Amen

STEP 9: *Made Direct Amends*

Here we take the bull by the horns and complete the process of clearing up our past. Here is Step 9: *Made direct amends to such people where ever possible, except when to do so would injure them or others.* Next we present a definition taken from *Light in the Darkness* by St George Lee, MD, page 25-26:

"Amends, taken in a general sense, are repairs for damage. Making amends refers to your taking responsibility for your part in pain that another has.

Let us consider what does not constitute making amends. Making amends is not asking for forgiveness. It is not trying to explain our actions. Nor is it taking responsibility for all of another's pain. Rather, making amends is simply an acknowledgment of the role you might have played in another's pain (and making it right).

Authentic amends do not depend on the type of response of the person to whom you make them. Whether the individual to whom you make amends thinks you are responsible for none of his pain or all of his pain is irrelevant to your amends. True amends result from an honest attempt to examine (and correct) how you have fallen short in interacting with others.

It is important to understand that making amends is a process and not a one-time event. You make amends authentic by future actions that back up the words you speak. The words are just a beginning. Authentic amends have little to do with the words themselves. Words may be empty. Actions do speak louder than words. The intention expressed in spoken or written words, on the other hand, is an appropriate way to *begin* the process of amends."

Thank you George.

17) Choose one of the following feelings (by circling) that you identify with or add your own feeling(s) to the lists if not included:

Making direct amends

Confident   Apprehensive   Vague   Hopeful

Fearful   Sincere   Guilty   Shameful

Facing people I have harmed

Scared   Dreadful   Relieved   Sad

Facing those who have harmed me

Angry   Sad   Fearful   Shameful

Possibly paying back money

Indifferent   Fearful   Shameful   Guilty   Calm

Have I considered making amends to myself?

Indifferent   Surprised   Curious   Relieved

Do I have a problem with making amends to the dead?

Vague   Fearful   Sad   Indifferent

Do I fear being blamed or rejected?

Fearful   Hopeful   Angry   Apprehensive

14) In the above questions, which three feelings showed up most frequently?

a) _____

b) _____

c) _____

Using your Step 8 list of amends as reference, answer the following questions:
15) Name the most difficult amends you believe you have to make.

_____

16) Name the least difficult.

_____

17) Explain how you think best to approach both in question three and four.

   a) _____

      _____

      _____

      _____

      _____

   b) _____

      _____

      _____

      _____

      _____

18) Are you able to make direct amends (face to face) or will you need to make indirect contact first?

      _____

      _____

      _____

      _____

      _____

_____

19) Is there someone deceased involved in your amends process? If so how best would you approach this amends? (Write a letter to them and God, visit the grave etc.).

_____

_____

_____

_____

_____

_____

20) We begin to make amends to ourselves and our immediate families by staying sexually sober and by working the steps but we don't stop there. Who in your family have you done the most harm (if listed in question 7 name another)?

_____

21) What do you believe is the best way to right your wrongs concerning them?

_____

_____

_____

_____

_____

22) If money is involved what do you think is the best way to proceed in making restitution (pay back money or property) to those you've harmed? Name two ways you think best to proceed before making the amend (Write a letter, phone call etc.).

a) _____

_____

_____

_____

_____

_____

b) _____

_____

_____

_____

_____

_____

23) If it were you that someone stole from or mishandled money, how would you like amends be made to you? This may help bring perspective to your money amends.

_____

_____

_____

_____

_____

_____

○ For any amends (repair of damages) we state what we did (our part in it), we make restitution as it applies (arrange to pay back money or restore property, stop having affairs, be emotionally available to those around you etc.). We make a commitment to them of what changes in our behavior we are going to implement in order not to display the same behavior again. We, as sex addicts, often haven't always taken the higher ground. We tend to brush things underneath the carpet. We must humble ourselves but we do not grovel. We maintain our dignity without false pride.

24) Humans are not the only ones we have put through the ringer. We may have harmed pets or other wildlife. If this is true for you, what will you do to correct this problem?

_____

_____

_____

_____

_____

_____

If we have damaged property and you don't know who it belonged to, we find ways to give back by donating to a worthy cause perhaps.

25) If this is true of you, what will you do to make amends?

_____

_____

_____

_____

26) Name the person who did you most harm, tell what your part in it was and how you will proceed? How did you react?

_____

_____

_____

_____

_____

_____

27) Do you owe yourself amends? The answer is yes. How do you propose to give ongoing amends to yourself (getting sober and working the steps being first, expanding your growth area etc.)? Name more.

_____

_____

_____

_____

_____

28) How are you going to make amends to your children?

_____

_____

_____

_____

29) In the case of STD's given to you or transmitted by you, how are you going to approach this?

_____

_____

_____

_____

_____

_____

30) If you have acquired a sexual disease like AIDS or herpes what measures will you take to prevent harming a partner (tell a potential partner long before sexual intimacy is involved etc.)?

_____

_____

_____

_____

_____

_____

31) If incest is involved (you as perpetrator or victim) what is your best course of action?

_____

_____

_____

_____

32) If there is someone from you 12 Step meetings you owe amends to, what are the positives and negatives of making this amend?

_____

_____

_____

_____

_____

_____

The Amends Process

We have gone over the list of amends with our sponsor during the 8th Step. During that step we agreed on the person or institution and exactly what amends would be made. We now take them *one amends at a time.*

The phrase *to such people where ever possible* will be discussed now. If we owe money we pay it back or make appropriate arrangements to pay. We take account of our present situation. We make arrangements to pay back money owed because of theft or mishandling. We don't exonerate ourselves because of extenuating circumstances, but at the same time if we have a family we also try not to penalize them unduly. We may be divorced and are behind on child support. We make arrangements to catch up on that support. If the mother of our children is involved with another individual, we cautiously approach the mother. We make indirect contact first and seek their permission to approach them to discuss the matter before proceeding. We are attempting to avoid harming others as we make amends. We pray and we take care of any anger or resentment before proceeding.

Suppose we have padded our account. If we go directly to our boss and confess our sin we may stand a chance of being fired. On the other hand, we know that we could act out again if we don't clear this matter up. So, we approach this situation cautiously but with the willingness to correct it. There are no hard and fast rules in such a delicate matter. We talk it over with our sponsors and family before we act. It is possible that we will be allowed to pay back mishandled funds or if we have been stealing time we may work additional hours with no pay for a period of time. We use our best judgment but we are sure to clear our debt in some way. We do what we can to mend our past wrongs.

If we have shoplifted, we pay the merchants back the money we owe them. We may have shoplifted or stolen from an employer from a business that has closed down. If so, we estimate to the best of our ability what we owe and perhaps make a contribution to a favorite charity or cause. One person shared that they went to a former business and attempted to pay the money back. The management had changed hands and the new owners were dumbfounded about what our friend was attempting to do. They discussed the matter and decided that they couldn't take the money. Our friend talked it over with her sponsor and decided to give the money to a local orphanage.

3) Choose the following (by circling yes or no) to identify your feelings about:

Am I fearful of retaliation?   Yes   No   Doesn't apply

Am I fearful of incarceration?Yes   No   Doesn't apply

Minors involved (fearful)?   Yes   No   Doesn't apply

Confident making amends?   Yes   No   Doesn't apply

Relieved by making amends? Yes   No   Doesn't apply

The phrase *when to do so would injure them or others* comes next. We use caution here when dealing with amends that could potentially harm others (ourselves included). We don't shy away from tough amends though. Remember that in Step 8 we became willing to make amends to <u>all</u> on our list. We just need to figure out the best way to approach each.

Most amends do not involve money, but deal with people we have harmed on a physical, emotional or intellectual level. We may have had an affair with someone's significant other. Do we go to that person and confess all? If they are unaware of the affair, you may harm one or both of them in doing so. In such a case we may simply want to stay away from the person we acted out with as our amends to both parties. If the person we harmed is a minor we may want to seek professional help in dealing with this delicate issue. It may not be wise to approach that person directly. Most importantly, we stop the behavior and stop contact with the person we've harmed.

There may be cases in which disclosure of certain information could result in our arrest. If illegal activity is still going on, first we stop that behavior and seek personal counseling (and perhaps legal counseling) to help us decide how to proceed. We keep our families and others in mind as well.

We go to any length to work our program but we are considerate of others. We don't save our own necks at the expense of others. We use prayer in all of the amends we are considering. We pray for willingness to stop our past behaviors and we pray for guidance in how best to proceed. Our sponsor's input is always welcome.

Are there STDs (sexually transmitted diseases) involved? If so we will have to disclose our problem if our sexual encounters exposed others to the STD's. One member shared this: "I was married. When I went out and drank I had affairs. I had acquired herpes in my escapades and I didn't know if I had given it to my boyfriend. Since the encounters were anonymous and I didn't know who the other people were, the only one I knew I could make this disclosure to was my significant other. My sponsor said that I shouldn't disclose details to him but only to say that during my drinking I had been sexual, acquired herpes, and it would be prudent for him to see a doctor. He took it hard but got it checked out and the doctor found no problems. Later the truth came out about the extent of my acting out. At the time I was concerned about possibly infecting him, what I told him seemed acceptable."

What if we were angry or resentful at someone and they had no knowledge of it? We may want to take the approach of getting to know them first and then when the time is right let them know that we had been resentful (or jealous, etc. without telling them specifics). Sometimes we use specific details as a hammer to beat up on the person we have problems with. If this is the case we find it better not to disclose details but to share generally about our fault in the matter. If resentment is our problem then we may let them know that we have been resentful towards them in the past, and that in the future we will talk about things that bother us instead of holding anger towards them.

Suppose there was incest done to you or by you when you were a child? Dealing with such matters may take a lot of time and prayer. We speak with our sponsor, develop a game plan to make the amends or to gain closure. Often we may choose to seek professional help as well. We consider those involved so as not to make matters worse. One person shared that they had molested their younger sister when they were children. They prayed about it and shared their fears but eventually brought the subject up with their sibling and the matter was resolved over coffee.

The person that we owe amends to may be deceased or incapacitated so that we can't make direct amends. We may want to write a letter and go to the grave site and read it. Some have read this letter to their sponsor or to God and then burned it. We ask others in recovery for suggestions. One person shared this: "I had resentment about a boy from my childhood. He was later killed in a war. I still clung to my resentment of him. On one occasion I was visiting the memorial wall in Washington DC and I was drawn to find his name on that wall. When I found it I got a pencil and piece of paper and rubbed it until the etching transferred an image of his name onto the paper. I put this paper in my wallet and forgot about it. Some months later I visited my home town where I was born. Our grade school had burned down and I proceeded to walk through the ruins. I now call this *walking through the ashes of my past.* I decided to visit the boy's mother. When I went to her house I remembered the paper with her son's name on it. I gave that piece of paper to her and my resentment vanished at that moment. It hasn't returned". In this instance this recovering sex addict became willing to make his amends in Step 8 and his Higher Power arranged an appropriate time, place and forum in which to do so . This is God at work *doing for us what we could not do for ourselves.* What is a miracle? A miracle is: When God chooses to remain anonymous.

There are many different types of amends that will come up that seem not to have a clear way to deal with them. We pray, we speak with others, and above all we stay willing to complete our work of making direct amends to those we have harmed and not cause more harm as we proceed. Some may not want you to continue with your amends and that it is OK. We have made a sincere attempt and that's all that counts. We let it go. Why do we go through this process and possibly suffer pain in our efforts? We do this to unblock our channel to God and to have lasting sobriety and this is the reason for working all of the 12 Steps.

Will everyone accept our amends? Probably not. That's OK. We go into our amends with sincere willingness not to assign blame but to *clear off our side of the street.*

The Big Book of Alcoholics Anonymous speaks about the promises we will receive. It states that 'during this phase our development we will be amazed before we are half way through.' This implies is that the full affect of the promises will begin to surface in our lives *half way through Step 9 of making our amends to others*. AA is the template for 12 Step recovery form sexual addiction.

Made Direct Amends

We initially make our amends, making arrangements and seeing each person face to face where possible. While we should not delay in making our amends, we don't force ourselves on others either. We work out what is best for both parties. Our goal is to clear our conscious of the wrongs we have done, but not at the expense of others. This initial phase of making amends may take several weeks or even months to complete. There are some we may have to do at a later time because of distance, economics, or availability.

If we get stumped or have fears about a particular amends, we recite the 8th Step Willingness Prayer until we have the willingness and we figure out what the appropriate amend is.

The principle of Step 9 is: AMENDMENT.

We continue to stay willing and we continue making amends as we go on to the 10th Step. Take time now for a relaxation meditation break.

KJ Nivin

Process of Sexual Recovery

PART 5: THE MAINTENANCE STEPS
Steps 10, 11 & 12

Process of Sexual Recovery

STEP 10

_____

KJ Nivin

CHAPTER 10

STEP 10

Continued Our Inventories

A pattern develops as we work each step. When we need willingness we pray for it and when action is required we consult others for input on how best to proceed.

Step 10 is the combination of the first nine steps. Instead of clearing up our past as we did in Step 1 through 9, this step is used to *clear up our present*. We still use prayer to find willingness and we use others' input for actions we need to take. Step 10 deals with the present. When present matters need to be cleared up, we already have the experience of working the first nine steps to help us. We work Step 10 by using a mini-version of the same procedures we used in the first nine steps. Step 10 reads: *Continued to take personal inventory and when we were wrong promptly admitted it.*

In working the first three steps of our 12 Step program we use this simple phrase: *I can't; He can; I think I'll let Him.* In the 1st Step we admit that we are powerless to stop our disease (I can't). In the second step, we realize a Higher Power can help us (He can). In Step 3 we decide to turn our life over to this power (I think I'll let Him). So, when we have issues in our present life, we work the first nine steps on the current problem just as we did on past issues. Here is an example:

Jill had a situation come up with a coworker/friend. Rumor had it that her coworker was bucking for promotion and that she had told Jill's boss something that would put Jill out of running for that position. Jill was burned up. Her anger turned into resentment (anger rethought). Jill began mistreating her friend. She would snub her and make comments that hurt her friend. Jill did her journaling at night and saw this negative pattern developing. She knew that to stay with her new way of life in recovery she needed to change her ways in this instance. She called her sponsor for input. She prayed and decided to take her own inventory to see where she was at fault. She discussed what she found (the resentments and mean-spirited mistreatment of her friend) and shared it in her recovery meeting. This action on her part takes her through the first five steps so far. Later that night she wrote in her journal and discovered her character flaws of self-centeredness and fear. She asked her Higher Power to remove the defects of character that she discovered (Steps 6 and 7). The next day Jill mustered up as much courage as she could manage and approached her coworker. Jill admitted that she had been resentful toward her friend and admitted she was wrong (the 8th and 9th Step). She also told her friend that in the future she intends to speak with her first before jumping to conclusions. (I worked for Father Martin at Ashley Drug and Alcohol Treatment Center for a time and he used to say: My favorite indoor sport is "Jumping to conclusions"). Her friend told her that that she, herself, wasn't eligible for the position and that there were rumors floating around. Her friend assured her that she hadn't said anything and this matter was cleared up that day. The 10th Step works if we work it. Jill had to get her hurt pride out of the way by working her recovery program and using the spirit of the first nine steps that are incorporated into the 10th Step to regain some balance and reestablish peace within and without. Why? So she could have more serenity and also remain sexually sober and not risk going back to using sex to cope with life's trials.

Recovering sex addicts who have not cleared up similar situations on a day-to-day basis risk going back into active addiction. It is necessary to integrate the 10th Step into our life on a daily basis; simple, right? Maybe, but it depends on how we have integrated the first nine steps. It will take practice to correct these day-to-day snafus.

On the next two pages you will find a suggested 10th Step inventory *checklist*. This checklist may be used as a daily or a weekly tool to develop self-honesty and to make amends as necessary. Use this chart to see if there are any recent amends owed or behaviors that need changing. We exchange our debits for our credits. As we practice constructive behaviors (credits) on a daily basis we move away from our destructive behaviors (debits). This exercise was practiced in working the 7th Step in this workbook.

Go through the checklist on the next two pages and see where you stand spiritually today. This is a way to measure your spiritual health.

Daily/Weekly Inventory Sheet

Debits		Credits	
Aggressive	_____	Assertive	_____
Co-dependent	_____	Assured	_____
Controlling	_____	Allowing	_____
Critical	_____	Supportive	_____
Dishonest	_____	Honest	_____
Disloyal	_____	Loyal	_____
Egotistical	_____	Humble	_____
Envious	_____	Grateful	_____
Fearful	_____	Courageous	_____
Gluttonous	_____	Moderate	_____
Gossiping	_____	Understanding	_____
Greedy	_____	Generous	_____
Guilty	_____	Guiltless	_____
Irritable	_____	Polite	_____
Jealous	_____	Accepting	_____
Judging	_____	Non-Judging	_____

Debits		Credits	
Lustful	_____	Loving	_____
People Pleasing	_____	Self-Assertive	_____
Perfectionistic	_____	Balanced	_____
Prejudiced	_____	Tolerant	_____
Proud	_____	Humble	_____
Resentful	_____	Forgiving	_____
Revengeful	_____	Sympathetic	_____
Selfish	_____	Giving	_____
Self-Centered	_____	God-Centered	_____
Self-Hating	_____	Self-Accepting	_____
Self-Pitying	_____	Grateful	_____
Slothful	_____	Motivated	_____
Stubborn	_____	Willing	_____
Undependable	_____	Dependable	_____
Worry (Full Of)	_____	Faithful	_____

How did you do? Remember: progress, not perfection. With practice it gets better; we strive for balance, not extremes. In time our assets (credits) take the place of our defects (debits). We may add new behaviors to our list when we find them or eliminate character flaws that have been removed.

Here are some questions that focus on today's experiences. Please answer each question as it relates to your present life (day-to-day).

1) There are several types of inventories we can add to our 10th Step. Do you have concern about performing a daily or weekly inventory? Explain.

_____

_____

_____

_____

_____

_____

2) We can choose when to do a spot-check inventory (making of mental notes) as long as we do it regularly. Am I willing to develop the habit of self-searching by using a spot-check inventory during the day?
   (Yes) (No)

3) As our day passes we may make mental notes (spot-check ourselves), looking especially for any of our character defects. Also we make note of our assets for balance. Name two ways you intend to implement and practice this new habit.

   a) _____

   _____

   _____

   _____

_____

_____

b) _____

_____

_____

_____

_____

4) The daily/weekly inventory of our debits (character defects) and our credits (constructive character traits) goes a step further than a spot-check inventory and is an excellent tool for helping us to see where we may owe amends (we write this at night). Am I willing to practice this type of inventory on a regular basis in working Step 10? Why or why not?

_____

_____

_____

_____

_____

As recovering sex addicts we may want to go on a spiritual retreat and do an annual or semi-annual 4th and 5th Step (make a moral inventory and tell our sponsor what we found) as part of our 10th Step. If we feel pressed, we meditate on this matter and seek answers for ourselves. The point in doing any 10th Step work is to develop a committed effort that fits our life. The above suggestions are examples of how we might approach this vital part of our recovery.

We keep ourselves on the path of sexual sobriety by using daily spot-checks, then at night write down what we found. For our annual or semi-annual inventories (Some use support speaking commitments in their home groups or other sexual recovery groups as a way of doing an annual inventory). After we *take our inventory* we proceed with making any amend we may owe. We do this in a timely manner, not waiting too long before we act but acting with balanced determination. We seek guidance from our sponsor or other recovering sex addicts and then we make our amends for today.

The principle of Step 10 is: VIGILANCE.

We work Step 10 on a regular on going basis.

Assignment: **You may copy your daily/weekly inventory checklist onto note cards, carry them with you and make a check on any item that comes up during the day This is your spot check inventory. You may want to laminate this sheet, use erasable markers and fill it out at the end of the day instead. Whatever you decide to do, "keep it simple." Write about what you find in your journal. Use your daily/weekly inventory as a spirituality check. We develop our own system as long as this part of our program is in place. We do need to *work* our program, and this is an important part of doing that. In time, many find this a valuable tool and they would not miss the time spent performing this self-check. Practice this for several weeks until you find out what works for you and continue this process of your recovery.**

These three last steps are called the maintenance steps. Step 10 is used to keep our emotions in line. In the next step we seek contact with our Higher Power. We move now to Step 11.

STEP 11

CHAPTER 11

STEP 11

Seeking Contact

Step 11 is our prayer and meditation step: *Sought through prayer and meditation to improve our conscious contact with God as we understood God, praying only for knowledge of His will for us and the power to carry that out.* We have indirectly practiced this step all along as we worked through the previous steps. Now we will search for ways to improve that contact with our Higher Power, aligning our will with God's.

Prayer

Prayer in most of the 12 Step programs is defined as *talking* with God and meditation is considered to be *listening*. Just think if we interacted with our bosses at work by only talking and not paying any attention to what their desires for us were. We may not last too long and be minus an employer. It is similar with our Higher Power. We need to communicate to God what is going on in our lives and then listen to what God is trying to communicate back to us. (This may sound strange to some.) We must concede that something greater than ourselves is at work in our lives. Whatever That May Be is keeping us from the behaviors we used to indulge in. If this is true, then it would be prudent to get to know this Friend more intimately.

Back in Steps 2 and 3 we became clear about our belief in a power greater than ourselves and we made a decision to turn our will and our life over to that power. Step 11 is a continuation of that process. We improve on what we've started. How do we improve anything? We make it more *user friendly*. If we have learned prayers on our journey through the proceeding steps, then we begin to find quiet times to read more spiritual literature and develop further in a spiritual sense.

There are many different forms of prayer. Now we expand our knowledge about the areas of prayer we have chosen and we look further to other forms of prayer. As long as we consider our Higher Power a loving, guiding force, we will do well to improve our contact with this power.

Meditation

Meditation can be made more powerful by researching meditation techniques developed by those who have practiced it for years. In this workbook we practiced a simple form of meditation. We relaxed our bodies and took a deep breath and slowly let it out and relaxed. Then we concentrated on quieting our minds. We took that further by going into a quiet place in our minds and relaxed mentally and spiritually. This simple technique can be expanded as well. We may use it as our basic preparation for other forms of meditation or we may just want to keep it simple and use the technique already learned.

Another form of meditation involves a quieting technique followed by visualizations. We let go of our thoughts and visualize a calm setting, such as a mountain scene or a setting by a lake or any other setting that appeals to us. These mental images may begin to replace the old familiar fantasies we were used to. We clean up our fantasies by use of positive visualizations. After we get used to practicing this, we perhaps go a step further by thinking of one of our prayers and meditating on its deeper meaning by breaking it down into each segment. Then we quiet ourselves again and listen --- just be. We don't worry about what we are listening for. We just practice listening. This may, in time, help us to become better listeners to others in our lives. There is always a practical side to what we are doing in spiritual exercises. As we stated in the past, "keep it simple sweetheart". We don't want to complicate something that is meant to be simple.

Our position may be sitting, lying down, walking or jogging. Whatever works best for us.

Answer the following questions about prayer and meditation using your experience so far. Think about what results you may want out of practicing contact with God.

1) Describe techniques of prayer and meditation you have been using while working the steps.

Prayer _____

_____

_____

_____

_____

_____

_____

Meditation _____

_____

_____

_____

_____

_____

2) Are you comfortable with these techniques? Explain.

_____

_____

_____

_____

_____

3) What type of results do you experience from prayer and meditation (calmness of body and mind, peace, serenity, knowledge of God's will etc.)?

_____

_____

_____

_____

_____

_____

4) Do you have *sources* of prayers and spiritual readings or have you heard others share some that might be helpful to you (religious books, recovery material, prayer techniques etc.)? There are also 11th Step meetings dedicated to practicing meditation with prayer.

_____

_____

_____

_____

_____

_____

5) Name three prayers that are helpful to you now (e.g., the Serenity Prayer, the Prayer of St. Francis, etc.).

a) _____

b) _____

c) _____

6) There are many meditation techniques that may be used for the purpose of relaxation and spiritual growth. Have you discovered or have you heard someone share about techniques that employ elements that bring about both relaxation and spiritual growth? Name two.

a) _____

_____

b) _____

_____

7) Some combine prayer and meditation and report powerful results. If you are not already combining these, explain how you might go about doing so. If you are doing so explain your technique.

_____

_____

_____

_____

_____

_____

8) Do you have fears associated with meditating or expanding your meditation practice?

_____

_____

_____

_____

_____

The next part of Step 11 is about *praying only for knowledge of God's will for us and the power to carry that out.* Some of us have been self-centered in our prayer to God. We want what we want when we want it. Some have practiced a lifetime of asking our Higher Power *for things* instead of seeking spiritual growth. Our main goal at this point is to refocus our energies on asking for *knowledge* of God's will for us and on seeking ways to do God's will in all our life. We begin to see that we have previously been children in a spiritual sense. God's will for me is simple: He wants me to stay sober and to help others in recovery. God also wants me to grow spiritually and this requires me to keep my life in the framework of the 12 Steps. This takes a lot of effort on my part and a lot of change. One sponsor told me that the only thing I had to change was everything in my life.

The question may come up: How can I stop asking for things I really need? If God is all knowing and is all caring, then God is way ahead of us. Suppose several of us wanted a new car and prayed for it. Some of us then got one and some didn't. What would our thinking be? Some would think that God had really blessed them and others may think that they were forgotten. We have certainly wasted a lot of time with these kinds of prayers. In Step 11 we take these questions out of our mental vocabulary (or thought process) by asking only for what God wants for us. Instead of focusing on our wants, we simply ask God to take care of us. This is real faith, which practiced on a regular basis, sets the stage for spiritual growth. Any material progress we may experience is usually always proceeded by spiritual growth.

Our aim now is to get to know what our creator wants most for us. If God is all powerful then we may shortchange ourselves by asking for something that would fall far short of God's will for us. We may ask for a car while God wants us to become race car drivers. (We can add anything else into this equation and still come up short.) It is in our best interest that we voluntarily submit to the humble position of being the student and allowing God to be our teacher.

We are at a deciding point in Step 11. Keeping that in mind, answer the following questions about finally turning our entire lives over to our Higher Power, allowing God to lead us to better places-spiritual places.

9) Do I have fears of turning my will and life (thoughts and decisions) entirely over to the care of God as I understand God? Name them.

_____

_____

_____

_____

_____

_____

10) Am I now or have I in the past asked for mostly what I want instead of what God wants for me? (Yes)   (No)

11) What kind of things have I asked for?

_____

_____

_____

_____

_____

_____

12) If you were to decide to pray for knowledge of God's will for you, how would your pray? If you're already doing this explain how you proceed.

_____

_____

_____

_____

13) Have you asked your sponsor or other people in recovery their experience? Explain.

_____

_____

_____

_____

_____

14) Have you read recovery literature on the 11th Step and the Twelve Traditions? List the materials.

_____

_____

_____

_____

_____

Assignment: Research two other prayers and two meditation techniques that you may choose to implement into your 11th Step process. Prayer techniques take into consideration the time, place and method we use for our prayer time. You may use any prayer you choose during this regularly scheduled period. Examples of group meditation are: Going on a spiritual retreat that practices silence or joining a Yoga group or an 11th Step group. There are many other possibilities. Find what works best for you. Above all find a place you won't be disturbed and a place you can relax comfortably. Practice Prayer and Meditation on the following page. Use the relaxation technique to relax yourself that you used in previous chapters before you begin the meditation.

Meditation

<u>Intro.</u>
Today - together, we can become part of something bigger than all of us. This happens naturally when we learn to take risks and also share our strength as well as our human faults with others who are like ourselves.

_____

We learn how to do this by going to meetings and practicing listening to others. Listening and waiting for a message. Of them many messages we hear, all of a sudden one seems to fit miraculously into the misshapen holes that run through our hearts and minds.

"I didn't know how to tell people that I was crazy", was one of those messages I received in a 12 Step meeting. The person who delivered this message wasn't speaking directly to me, but he might as well have been. He was in fact recalling for the group, how he had felt when he was two years sober in the Fellowship.

Through this ordinary member taking a risk and sharing his "extraordinary" thoughts and feelings, a wonderful bond was created. What was once a personal struggle for him and for myself was now a part of the collective consciousness of the group. I knew that I didn't have to act <u>normal to belong</u> at that table. I only needed to practice honesty, open-mindedness and the willingness to learn to speak what's in my heart.

Affirmation.
Today, I will practice being a part of my Fellowship. I will find gratitude as I listen to others share and look for the courage to share my story with them.

Prayer
Dear God,

  Thank you for another day and yet another opportunity to learn and grow. Thank you for the sunlight that stirs my soul and warms my heart.
Amen_____

Written by a Recovering-12 Step Fellowship Member Lee E.

We proceed into the 11th Step with balance in mind.

The principle of Step 11 is: ATTUNEMENT.

We don't become extreme or excited in approaching this new way of life. And this *is* a new way of life for us. How many of us, before we started our recovery, have asked only for knowledge of our Higher Power's will and sought to carry that out? As we begin to get deeper into our recovery we begin to pass on to others what was freely given to us, and our lives continue to change in ways that we would never have thought possible. We enter into a new way of life, a way that will help others to recover from sex addiction. It aligns us with our Higher Power and those around us. We become attuned to our surroundings, instead of lurching, life begins to flow. We become at peace with our environment and ourselves. We are calm when chaos is going on all around us. We begin to notice that we are changing. This is the power of the 11th Step. We begin to meditate on a regular basis.

A form that I use daily I call Quiet Time where I sit where I won't be disturbed and Listen to God. I do this early in the morning at the same time each day. I have a small note book and pen and I write everything I hear...Good, Bad, and In between. I don't debate what I hear but when I finish I use the four standards HULP: if what I wrote is absolutely Honest, Unselfish, Loving, and Pure it is very possible it is from God. I also talk what I wrote down with someone who is doing the same. The process is described in the book "*How to Listen to God*" by Wally Paton. This method was used by early AA's in the 1930's and 40's. It works-it really does.

This takes us to Step 12.

STEP 12

CHAPTER 12

STEP 12

Spiritual Awakening

We have now come to our goal in the program.

The principle of Step 12 is: SERVICE.

Our goal in working the 12 Steps is to get and stay sober and then pass on to others what has so freely been given to us. We are free. Not free of our responsibility but free to start a life based on spiritual principles. We have a new responsibility.

Step 12 may be written as: *Having had a spiritual awakening as the result of these steps, we tried to carry this message to other sexually compulsive addicts and to practice these principles in all aspects of our lives.* Notice we underlined the word *the*. We emphasize this because this spiritual awakening did not come as "*a*" result of the steps and "*a*" result of anything else, but our awakening came as "*the*" direct result of working through and integrating the 12 Steps into our every day lives. We are grateful for AA and its gift of the 12 Step program (and for the 12 Principles), a gift that was passed down to our sexual addiction recovery programs. We are grateful for the "S" programs (sexual addiction programs) and other 12 Step programs that guide us in our recovery.

If you look back to when you started the 1st Step and how you felt then, you might agree that in working through this process you have gained spiritual tools that have changed your way of thinking and behaving, including spiritual awakening. You also have begun a lifetime of practicing these principles you have learned to apply to every aspect of your life. What are the principles? As mentioned in previous chapters:

Principles of the 12 Steps

Step 1: SURRENDER

Step 2: HOPE

Step 3: COMMITMENT

Step 4: HONESTY

Step 5: TRUTH

Step 6: WILLINGNESS

Step 7: HUMILITY

Step 8: REFLECTION

Step 9: AMENDMENT

Step 10: VIGILANCE

Step 11: ATTUNEMENT

Step 12: SERVICE

We *surrender* to the recovery process. We find *hope* in a Higher Power and then we *commit* to that hope. We get *honest* with ourselves and others and then tell the *truth* about our disease. We become *willing* to face our defects and then we *humbly* ask for their removal. We *reflect* on harm done and then make *amends* to those we've harmed. We stay *vigilant* working the program. We *attune* ourselves to our Higher Power and then preform His work of *service* to others.

These principles are the *short version* of the 12 Steps. These are the principles we practice when we utilize the steps in our every day lives. Our new life leads to the final step; the 12th Step of service to God and others. We stop praying only for what we want for ourselves and pray more for others (we don't pray for what we want for them, we pray for God's will for them). We throw ourselves into service work *for* others. We benefit greatly when we *help out*. There are many ways for us to be of service.

Define the 12 Principles

In the following exercise keeping in mind service work is a part of our program now. Write your own definition of each principle below as it applies to your program.

1) Surrender:

_____

_____

_____

_____

_____

2) Hope:

_____

_____

_____

_____

_____

3) Commitment:

_____

_____

_____

_____

_____

4) Honesty:

_____

_____

_____

_____

_____

_____

5) Truth:

_____

_____

_____

_____

_____

6) Willingness:

_____

_____

_____

_____

_____

7) Humility:

_____

_____

_____

_____

_____

_____

8) Reflection:

_____

_____

_____

_____

_____

_____

9) Amendment:

_____

_____

_____

_____

_____

_____

10) Vigilance:

_____

_____

_____

_____

_____

_____

11) Attunement:

_____

_____

_____

_____

_____

_____

12) Service:

_____

_____

_____

_____

_____

_____

We have learned the above principles by working the 12 Steps. Now we simply practice them. We begin to think of what we can do for the next suffering sex addict.

Service to Others

Service is a vital part of our program. We don't do service work to win any awards. We do it because it was done for us and it helps remind us how it was in our addiction, by working with newcomers. Other sex addicts gave us their time and patience so that we could attend a meeting by having the meeting there for us, to get and stay sexually sober through sponsoring us, and now we give back by passing this message of hope on to others by doing service work as well. When we sponsor someone it is in order to help us maintain close contact with the steps and to possibly help the suffering sex addict in the process. We emulate what our sponsor and others recovering sex addicts did for us. By doing service work, we find that we benefit more ourselves. First and foremost: *We are doing this for our own recovery.*

We never really finish our steps and that's where sponsorship comes in. When we take another sex addict through the process of working the steps for themselves, we rework them for ourselves. Many of us find more about our inventories than when we first worked the steps. More things come to the surface for us and we may freely talk to our sponsees and our support about what we find. We may even find we want to work the steps again with a different sponsor or on different issues that we find while working with others.

Examples of Service

There are many forms of service work besides sponsorship. We also may do these in addition to becoming a sponsor but remember balance. Bill W. of AA once said "We do many things poorly and one thing supremely." We can apply this to service work. We take one service commitment at a time as we sponsor others. It is important, however, to take a position in our group and share the load. Examples of types of service are:

Group Treasurer
GSR (Group Service Representative)
Secretary
Chairperson
Literature Person
Coffee Maker
Take calls from other less experienced sex addicts

Intergroup Chair
Intergroup Treasurer
Committee Member
Intergroup Secretary
Telephone Response Line Person
Regional Representative
Support structure on national and international levels

Read literature on the 12 Traditions for more information. It is necessary to become familiar with these traditions when we are involved in service work.

Answer the following questions:

13) Am I willing to be of maximum service to God and my fellows?   Yes   No

14) What are my reasons for doing service work or not doing it?

_____

_____

_____

_____

_____

_____

15) Have I seen anyone in my meetings that may need and want a sponsor?
(Yes) (No)

16) Remember this is a program of attraction. So we make ourselves available by speaking with newcomers before and after meetings. Have I started to give out my phone number or E-mail address to support a sex addict in recovery?
(Yes) (No)

17) Some sponsor others long distance via phone or E-mail. One such relationship was 4,000 miles apart. Am I willing to help someone even from a distance? (Yes) (No)

18) Is there a service position available in my home group that I could fill?
(Yes) (No)

19) Am I willing to help set the room up and make coffee if necessary?
(Yes) (No)

20) Am I concerned enough about a still suffering sex addict, inside or outside our rooms, to be available to help them? (Yes) (No)

There are many more questions that come to mind but it is important that we ask ourselves these and find the answers for ourselves. What will help my sobriety today?

We find resources available for sex addicts getting out of prison. Some will not hire them or allow them to live in their neighborhoods. We find treatment facilities and phone numbers in case these are needed. We do mail outs to Counseling Centers and churches to let them know that our meetings are available. There are many more effective ways to *pass it on*.

We hope this workbook has helped you get and stay sober but also we hope that it sparks an interest in you to help others: especially sex addicts.

Final Program Check

You have added more actions to your program of sobriety and now you have a program in place:

You are going to at least one meeting a week or receiving help with your addiction to sex.

You know who your sponsor is and are working with him or her on the 12 Steps. You now attend meetings on a regular basis and you have phone numbers of members in recovery from sexual addiction and are staying in regular contact.

You are reading recovery material and the meditation book *Answers in the Heart* on a regular basis.

You are journaling and writing a weekly stressor list and making mental note of your feelings.

You are making sobriety plans to get through the day without acting out and you are using the two circles. You are expanding your growth area of recovery.

You may have endured physical or emotional withdrawal or know how to deal with it and can pass that experience on to others.

You are practicing not reacting to negative situations and people and are relying on your Higher Power. You are abstinent from your addictive circle behaviors and you are stable.

You share your concerns with your support group and/or your sponsor? You are working the first three steps on a daily basis.

You have made an inventory of your grosser character flaws and shared them with your sponsor. You have made lists of good and bad traits and placed them on note cards and have checked them during the week? You have now worked Steps 4, 5, 6, and 7.

You have made a list of amends and have begun the process of making direct amends. You are working Step 8 and 9.

You have made a daily/weekly inventory list and use this list to make amends promptly when you were wrong. You now pray and meditate daily to overcome any negative defects of character that come up. You are now working Step 10 (which are a combination of steps 1 through 9) and Step 11. You'll find your final assignment follows:

> *Assignment:* **Here is your final assignment: Work Step 12 by helping another sex addict. Do this by sponsoring less experienced sex addicts on a regular basis because: There may come a time when all else fails to stop the urge to act out; helping another suffering sex addict can help assure that we stay addiction free. We are of maximum service to God and others. We pass on to others what was freely given to us.**

Just how far do we go? We go to any length and then *"One Step More"*
(Thank you Father Martin of Ashley)

KJ Nivin

Process of Sexual Recovery

KJ Nivin

EPILOGUE

REFLECTIONS

EPILOGUE

REFLECTIONS

Working The Program

During our process of working through and integrating the 12 Steps into our lives we have learned much. To review what we have accomplished: In Step 1 we defined our addiction and we learned about how stress and triggers could cause us to act out sexually. In the 2nd Step we identified our insanity and we came to believe that a power greater than ourselves could restore us to sanity. Step 3 was a continuation of the second step in that we decided to rely on God as we understand Him. We also decided to work the rest of the 12 Steps. In Step 4 we made an inventory of our grosser defects of character. We continued this process by admitting our wrongs to our sponsor during the 5th Step. In the 6th and 7th Steps we became willing and then asked our Higher Power to remove our character defects (shortcomings). Steps 8 and 9 completed the process of dealing with past wrongs done to people and institutions. First we became willing and then we made direct amends to those we offended. In Step 10 we combined all of the steps from Step 1 through 9 to deal with our present. We took our daily inventory and promptly admitted our wrongs. Step 11 is a continuation of Step 3. We began to have a relationship with our Higher Power by seeking God through prayer and meditation. The last step, Step 12, is the step in which we begin to do service work – service to God and our fellow man. This has only been the beginning of our recovery. *More will be revealed.*

Conclusion: After completing the 12 Steps we begin to look at the world around us in a different way, a more mature way. Some of us are able to hold on to our present relationships and some relations dissolve as we let go. We are grateful for what our Higher Power has given us, what has been taken away, and what is left.

Some of our wives or significant others have adapted to the idea that we are sex addicts. They know there is no cure and most understand the necessity of daily attention to our spiritual condition. Some will remain in denial. Our sobriety is contingent upon spiritual maintenance. The important thing is that we know and accept that we have a disease, a disease that will take everything we have, want or need, unless we attend to it on a daily basis.

We don't hide from our disease of sexual addiction; we embrace it. Yes, we do stay away from people, places and things that will seriously endanger our sobriety. There may be borderline situations that we feel we must be present for, and we do attend to those. The bottom line is that if we are triggered or believe that our environment will lead to acting out, we quietly excuse ourselves or we make other plans and arrangements.

Some will begin new relationships. We carry our program with us into our dating. We set internal boundaries for ourselves and we allow the other person to be who they are. If the relationship is unhealthy for us we move on and let go. We abstain from sexual contact until we are in a committed relationship. This may take six to nine months or a year to consider our union a committed relationship. Our goal is to get to know the person and allow them to know us. Sex may cover up defects of character in either party that may later potentially cause problems of incompatibility. We want to experience the other person without the chance of sexual censorship. This will help us to decide if we want to make further commitment as time passes.

Marriages are tough at times especially when trust has been broken. There may be children involved or other circumstances that can be difficult to work through. For married folk and people already in a committed relationship there is help for the partner of the sex addict and for the family as well. *This is a family disease*. There are recovery meetings available for the people in our lives. (See Appendix III). We encourage them to get help for themselves without badgering them.. We advise them as we would advise a friend. We let them know that recovery meetings are available for friends and family of recovering sex addicts and then we let the subject drop. We allow them to decide what they want to do. Remember that we have made a list of our character defects. One of those may be manipulation which can be very destructive. *We create our own space and we live in it.*

Counseling and treatment are available for sex addicts and their families. (Some are listed in Appendix III.) There are also workshops and facilitated groups that are available through counseling centers. We do what is necessary to overcome our compulsion for sexually acting out.

Milestones will show up as we recover. Some of these milestones are slow to materialize and some come in sudden events. We may begin a new career after working through the 12 Step process. We may exchange unhealthy relationships for healthy ones. We don't look for the right relationship we become the right relationship (let it begin with me). As time passes and trust is developed, our friends and family may see us in a new light. We may engage in a hobby or creative pastime that may become a new career or a life-changing experience for us. Some aspects of our life may fall away and are soon replaced by new healthy ones. Most of the time, others notice these milestones before we do. In journaling we will notice the changes taking place as we review our past notes.

Some may want to consider dual addiction. This refers to the co-existence of multiple addictions like sex addiction and alcoholism. Others that may show up with sexual addiction include compulsive overeating, gambling, illegal drug or prescription addiction, compulsive debting (time or money) and spending, nicotine addiction etc. These and other compulsive behaviors can be life-threatening and need immediate solution. Many of us have problems in these areas. When we find we have little or no control over them (i.e., that we are addicted), we must address them. These issues may create a vicious cycle of relapse. We let go of one form of addiction and replace it with another and eventually find ourselves back in our primary addiction. We find we need to attend to spiritual recovery in these other forms of addiction by working the 12 Steps and attending recovery meetings of that specific addiction.

With personal growth comes personal responsibility. We help our home groups and service organizations with providing service work and we help other sex addicts to achieve sexual sobriety by sponsorship. We do make sure there is no sexual attraction to those we help. Our motives must be pure: To help a suffering sex addict out of the trap of repetitive sexual compulsion. In return we will help ourselves. A rule of thumb: If we aren't helped by sponsoring someone (E.g., they only want to use us and aren't really interested in sobriety.) then we move on to someone willing to work through the 12 Steps with us. We look for progress in our sponsee. Do they do their home work and show up for sponsorship appointments? We don't hinder someone else's personal growth. We don't do for them what they should be doing for themselves. We may need to give them assistance in the beginning but shortly afterward the newcomer must begin to rely upon the God of their understanding. We don't play God. *They must suit up and show up.*

If we move or are geographically isolated we contact sexual recovery groups and get support. Contacts for these groups can be found on the Internet or through local counseling offices. We may obtain a sponsor who is many miles away from us who can fill the gap when meetings aren't available. We all need support in dealing with our problem. Two heads are better than one. Online groups exist that can give us a meeting in absentia.

Whatever we do we make the most of our new life that God has most graciously provided. We change our attitudes and look at the *cup half full*. We move forward and become good stewards of our sobriety. We pray and we meditate for God's will for us and for the power to carry that out. It is up to us what we do with our new gift: *The Circle Of Life - beyond the circles.*

AUTHORS' MESSAGE

How do you feel now after completing this work? I felt changed after working through the 12 Step process of recovery from sexual addiction with my Sponsor. I hope you do as well. I began to experience many changes the year after completing the 12 Steps.

My hope for you is that you will take what you experienced during your journey through the steps and pass it on to other suffering sex addicts.

It is my sincere intention to be of service to as many suffering sex addicts as possible. I have chosen to do so through the medium of sharing my sexual recovery program. This book was written from the viewpoint of being a sponsor as apposed to being a therapist or counselor. I have sponsored my share of people in recovery; in alcohol recovery for over 26 years, compulsive spending for over 10 years and sexual recovery for over 13 years. I have also attended codependency programs. I've performed many levels of service work in these fellowships but nothing compares to being a *sponsor* to a still suffering person and to watch that person change from a hopeless state to a life...valued.

I've heard some recovering people from other fellowships say "Sex addiction: That is the addiction to have." Of course they've never been there. We, as sex addicts, know the despair, the shame, and devastation that our compulsive sexual behaviors have brought to us. We wished for the end and the end did not come. Our addictive behavior continued. We were at the jumping off point and had no where to go. We tried to control or moderate but our acting out just got worse or took another turn into another dead end. Yes we know that this disease of sexual addiction can reap a deadly harvest on ourselves and our relationships.

I am sexually sober today by the grace of God my Higher Power. By God's grace I hope you can find a path of recovery that works for you. We don't merely have meetings to go to we are members of a *society of recovering people* and where ever we go we can find help and fellowship. *We are never alone.* Our addictions may all be different, but there is a common solution – the 12 Steps. Take these Steps and begin the journey with those who were before you, and we'll see you on the "Highway to happy destiny." See You Sober.

Sincerely, KJ NIVIN

STORIES

     In the Introduction we mentioned that we would be asking anyone who are interested, after working through this workbook, to send their personal stories. These stories would be greatly appreciated. We are publishing a book about post-addiction experiences. We want to know what happened in your lives as recovering sex addicts after working the 12 Steps. We believe that by integrating the 12 Steps into a recovering sex addict's daily life that many changes will occur. We are interested in those changes. We are interested in how you expanded your 'growth area" to enter "The Circle of Life."

     When writing your story, especially focus on your experience while working through this workbook and afterward. You may tell the story of your addiction before you began this process, but keep that part short if possible – five to seven pages. We would most like to know what happened once you started putting the 12 Principles of Recovery into practice and what items you have placed in your growth area to expand it. Tell us what emotional and spiritual changes have taken place, as well and what actions you have performed to enhance you recovery. Please share about your God experiences you may have had before, during, and after working the 12 Steps.

     Please send you stories or any comments about *The Circle of Life* to **kjnivin@yahoo.com**. (List any typographical errors found in this publication and send to this address as well…thank you)

Visit our website/blog at: https://sites.google.com/site/circleoflifesite/
http://kjnivin-circleoflife.blogspot.com/

Again, keep in mind that we reserve the right to edit any articles you send and that the articles will become the sole property of The Circle of Life author KJ NIVIN. Please send all stories typed, double spaced and please use English as the language.

APPENDIX I

The Master & The Camel

Miracles are not Mirages

A Good Master found a wandering Camel. The Camel was undernourished and looked unloved. And most of all it looked lost. From the marks on the Camel the Good Master could tell that the poor lost Camel's previous master had been cruel. The Good Master looked the Camel over and could only see the good traits in this pitiful beast even though the camel was in very poor condition. The Master thought to him self: "This camel will make a good servant and I will feed it and nourish it and soon I will have a good servant and the servant will have a purpose in life besides just wandering through the desert lost." Day by day the Good Master nursed and loved the Camel back to health. Soon the Camel felt better than he had ever felt but he still felt somewhat unsure of himself. After a time the Good master began to train the Camel. At first the Camel didn't like the idea of someone leading him around all day. There was some good that the Camel could see: The Good Master knew where all of the healthy watering holes were and he knew where the right kind of nourishing food was stored. And the Master never yelled, but whispered. The Camel began seeing the benefit of cooperating in this training even though he couldn't see where it was leading him. The Master taught him how to go without drinking for increasing longer distances, no more than one day though. That seemed like a long time but he began to get used to it.

The Master Never Gave Him
More Than He Could Carry

One morning the Good Master woke the Camel early and brought him to a place where there was a load of supplies. The Good Master knelt the Camel down and placed the appropriate load on his new servants back. At first the Camel thought that he could never carry all of that load but the Good Master knew he was now strong enough to carry the small load that looked so big to the Camel. They started out into the desert as usual and as they went along the Good Master showed him many things. Things that the Camel had not noticed before. And so it went.

The Master's Voice

The Master whispered to the Camel one day that his own Father had taught him all of these things and now it was up to him to teach the Camel how to be of service and to live properly. The Camel began to love the Master's quiet voice. That night the Good Master brought the Camel over to a nice rest area and knelt the Camel down and removed its load. The Camel was grateful that the load had been removed and soon after a good meal and fresh water, he fell off to sleep.

Bright and early the next morning The Master awakened the Camel. The Camel was grumpy. Hadn't I done enough the Camel thought. I've carried the huge load all day and now I have to carry it again today. The Good Master only smiled and patted the Camel on the back and said that the tiredness would pass soon and he would not even notice it later on in their journey. Just as the Master said, the day went by and he had forgotten all about the load and being so tired that morning and the Good Master had shown him such wonderful things along the way. How had he missed all of the beauty around him for so long?

The Purpose

Night was coming soon and he looked forward to the rest. This time however the Camel noticed that they were entering a town much like his own town that now seemed so far away. As he went in he noticed that many were gathered. They looked so happy to see the Good Master and even though they didn't know the Camel, they treated him just as the Good Master treated him. Some of the group members were glad to get the food and supplies that were brought. The Camel noticed that some of them looked as he had when the Good Master had found him. The Camel felt some pride in being of service to these good folks, especially the ones that looked so lost. The Camel thought: My, how my life has changed since I met the Good Master and just look at all of the friends I have had and didn't even know I had them until I was saved from my wandering.

That night as before the load was removed and the next morning the Camel awoke by himself without the Masters assistance. The Camel was surprised at himself. The next surprise came to the Camel when he noticed that he was kneeling before the Master & waited for the proper load to be placed on his back. This was OK now and it was so automatic and seemed second nature to him . He smiled to himself, he even looked forward to caring the load that day.

Never Alone

Later in the afternoon as they journeyed together the Master leaned close to the Camel and hugged him, patted him on the back and said: You have become a good servant. You know the way now and you know where the nourishing waters flow and you can go without a drink for 24 hours.

Now, go, my Good and Trusted Servant and bring food and supplies and nourishing waters to the many friends that you haven't met yet. They need what you have and you may now teach others to do the same. If you do get off the path, just call my name and I will be that still and small voice you hear to guide you.

In Sobriety,

KJ NIVIN. 04 Aug 1999

The Master & The Camel is a story of recovery - spirituality - about sponsorship, prayer, Higher Power, and passing the message of recovery on to others so they can do the same. This is how my Higher Power (God As I Understand God) found me and brought me back to life by allowing me to be sponsored through the 12 Steps and made me useful.

APPENDIX II

The original 12 Steps:

1. We admitted that we were powerless over alcohol-that our lives had become unmanageable.
2. Came to believe that a power greater than ourselves could restore us to sanity.
3. Made a decision to turn our will and our lives over to the care of God as we understood Him.
4. Mad a searching and fearless moral inventory of ourselves.
5. Admitted to God, to ourselves, and to another human being the exact nature of our wrongs.
6. Were entirely willing to have God remove all these defects of character
7. Humbly asked God to remove our shortcomings.
8. Made a list of all people we had harmed and became willing to make direct amends to them all.
9. Made direct amends to such people wherever possible except when to do so would injure them or others.
10. Continued to take personal inventory and when we were wrong promptly admitted it.
11. Sought through prayer and meditation to improve our conscious contact with
   God as we understood Him, praying only for His will for us and the power to carry that out.
12. Having had a spiritual awakening as the result of these steps, we tried to carry this message to alcoholics and to practice these principles in all our affairs.

Note: Alcoholics Anonymous, nor is any other 12 Step programs of recovery (to include DA, NA, GA, SLAA, SAA, SA, RCA etc), affiliated with this publication, or that it has read and/or endorses the contents thereof. A.A. is a program of recovery from alcoholism only-inclusion of the Steps in this publication, or use in any other non-A.A. context, does not imply otherwise. Additionally, while A.A. is a spiritual program, A.A. is not a religious program. Thus, A.A. is not affiliated or allied with any sect, denomination, or specific religious belief as are any other 12 Step program.

Additionally this entire statement of non-affiliation may also apply to any other 12 Step program. The following 12 Steps are generically written. These Steps and this workbook are not associated or affiliated with any Sexual Addiction Recovery Program:

Sexual Addiction 12 Steps:

1. We admitted that we were powerless over addictive sexual behavior and/or sexual compulsion-that our lives had become unmanageable.
2. Came to believe that a power greater than ourselves could restore us to sanity.
3. Made a decision to turn our will and our life over to the care of God as we understood Him.
4. Made a searching and fearless moral inventory of ourselves.
5. Admitted to God, to ourselves, and to another human being the exact nature of our wrongs.
6. Were entirely willing to have God remove all these defects of character
7. Humbly asked God to remove our shortcomings.
8. Made a list of all people we had harmed and became willing to make amends to them all.
9. Made direct amends to such people wherever possible except when to do so would injure them or others.
10. Continued to take personal inventory and when we were wrong promptly admitted it.
11. Sought through prayer and meditation to improve our conscious contact with God as we understood God, praying only for His will for us and the power to carry that out.

12. Having had a spiritual awakening as the result of these steps, we tried to carry this message to our fellow sex addicts and to practice these principles in all aspects of our lives.

APPENDIX III

Resources

Literature:

1. Alcoholics Anonymous - *Alcoholics Anonymous.*
2. Alcoholics Anonymous – *The Twelve Steps and the Twelve Traditions.*
3. Carnes, Patrick - *Out of the Shadows, Don't Call It Love, Facing the Shadow*
4. Friends in Recovery – *The Twelve Steps for Christians.*
5. Hunter, Mic – *Hope and Recovery*
6. Lee, St. George – *Light in the Darkness.*
7. Sex Addicts Anonymous – *Sex Addicts Anonymous.*
8. *Sex and Love Addicts Anonymous*
9. *Sexaholics Anonymous*
10. Brown, Bruce – *Understanding Twelve-Step Programs (A Quick Reference Guide)*

Treatment and counseling:

1. Keystone Center
2. Sierra Tucson
3. The Meadows
4. Sante Center for Healing
5. Del Amo Hospital
6. Promises Treatment Center
7. The Life Healing Center
8. Sexual Recovery Institute
9. Michael Bohan of Meridian Psychotherapy in Virginia Beach
10. St George Lee, Family Therapy Office, 18 J Clyde Morris Blvd, Newport News, Virginia 757-593-2363
11. Father Martins Ashley Drug and Alcohol Treatment Center, Havre de Grace, Md.
12. Full Spectrum Recovery & Counseling Services, Santa Barbara, CA.

12 Step Programs for sex addiction recovery:

1. Sex Addicts Anonymous
2. Sex and Love Addicts Anonymous
3. Sexaholics Anonymous
4. Recovering Couples Anonymous
5. Sexual Compulsives Anonymous
6. Survivors Incest Anonymous
7. COSA (Co-Sex Addicts Anonymous
8. S-ANON
9. Co-SLAA

KJ Nivin

THE CIRCLE Of LIFE
Workbook Recovery Series

Available:

The Circle of Life:

The Alcoholic Recovery Workbook

Compulsive Debting 12 Step Workbook

The Circle Of Life series was developed to help with the basics of recovery. A strong emphasis is placed on obtaining and utilizing a 12 Step program sponsor. We stress attendance of addiction support meetings specific to the addictive disease we have and developing a support system. The intention of these workbooks are to aid recovery from addiction. These workbooks do not address formal religion or dogma. This process of recovery, we believe through our own experience, is spiritual in nature and change through guidance of a Power greater than ourselves becomes the key to recovery.

See our website at: https://sites.google.com/site/circleoflifesite/

Available: Dying To Live (Boulevard of Broken Dreams)
The KJ Nivin Story

Available also: Novels and Short stories

KJ Nivin

.

ABOUT THE AUTHOR:

KJ Nivin (pseudonym) who wishes to remain anonymous has been sober and in recovery from Alcoholism for over twenty seven years, in recovery for fourteen years from sexual addiction, and compulsive debting/spending since the year 2000. He has worked through the 12 Step process for all three and for codependent behavior, the Steps for children of alcoholics, and for narcotics as well. He has sponsored many recovering alcoholics and other addicts by setting an example and integrating the steps into his own life. He now works with the recovery community to help families and friends.

He has a vast experiential knowledge by working for organizations such as Father Martin's Ashley drug and alcohol recovery center, with patients who are in treatment facilities in the Navy and US Army Drug and Alcohol Rehabilitation Programs, and other recovery programs.

Now retired from military service, he has traveled the world in recovery and practiced sobriety as a soldier as well as in Desert Storm. In being sober himself he has passed the message of recovery on to others by speaking to many recovery groups, TV news programs, Counseling Center staff members, Universities, and organizations interested in addiction.

He began his recovery from alcoholism in August 1983. He worked the steps with a sponsor and then began sponsoring others through the 12 Steps. He has written 12 Step Workbooks covering the subject matter of sexual addiction, alcoholism, and compulsive debting/spending.

KJ Nivin prefers spirituality over religion and has a God of his own understanding and from that relationship Nivin decided he could help others on a greater scale by publishing his workbooks...The Circle of Life workbook series. He has adopted the idea: "Don't let the good get in the way of the best," and recovering people need the best to stay in recovery.

KJ feels that, in this way, he can give back to his community and to mankind what was so freely given to him.

KJ Nivin

Made in United States
Cleveland, OH
09 January 2025